The House on Sackett Street
A Love Story

An EJM Romance Tale

Elizabeth J. McDonald

ISBN: 1479313130
ISBN-13: 978-1479313136

DEDICATION

To all the Marcias out there

Prologue

The long hell was finally over and the government men left the house. I was alone at last in my new home. Alone, at last, with my new identity, my new name, my new past, and my new future. I was happy...and sad.

I walked around the house for a while. It was filled with nice furniture, nice linens, and nice pictures on the wall. The living room was complete with a couch, two nice overstuffed chairs, and a wooden rocker. An oak wall unit completed the decor. In the kitchen were all my nice new cooking utensils, although some of them certainly did not look brand new. I guess that was for the image the government men gave me.

Over the hall bookcase was a photograph of me with a man. I was in a pretty bridal gown and appeared to be about twenty years younger. It was taken at the altar of a church. There was a lot of dark wood with a very impressive stained glass window behind the alter. I was carrying a bouquet of spring flowers and had some in my hair. The man, very good looking in a handsome blue and black tuxedo, stood next to me. We were both smiling. I remembered when that photo was taken. It wasn't twenty years ago.

Next to that photograph were two other pictures of a boy and a girl. They were high school graduation portraits. Below them were the same two, together with a man and a woman. I was the woman. The man, the same as the wedding portrait. They were all smiling, a nice looking house behind them with green grass and trees. A happy looking family.

Upstairs in the bedroom there was a queen sized bed, an oak dresser, a vanity, and a pair of wooden, lyre back chairs. The bedspread was of lilac flowers over a white, ruffled eyelet bed skirt. On the vanity was an assortment of cosmetics, perfumes, a hairbrush, and a pair of combs. A faint scent of various cosmetics and perfumes could be sensed. A pair of gold earrings and a silver necklace lay on top of a small hand mirror. In the bathroom were pretty pink and blue towels and matching bathmat and shower curtain. All very nice and very feminine, but with just a touch of a past male presence.

I looked into the full-length mirror on the wall. I saw what everyone else in the neighborhood had seen the past few days as I was moved into the house on Sackett Street. I saw a tall, middle-aged woman with just a touch of grey in her auburn hair. Her eyes were somewhat tired looking, but not sad. Her complexion, though not perfect, was acceptable. She wore large glasses that complemented her face and gave her a pleasant, friendly look. The oxford shirt, a bit too large, worn with the shirttails out, hid the fact that her breasts were somewhat large and a little saggy. The jeans showed that her hips were a bit full and her waist a little thick, but not as thick as she remembered it some months ago.

It was late afternoon, and I was tired and a bit dirty from the moving. I wanted to take a shower so I unbuttoned my shirt, threw it into the laundry hamper, and then slid my jeans down. Now, looking into the mirror I still did not believe what I saw. There was still that middle-aged woman. The simple white cotton bra held the breasts up. The stomach was a bit saggy and there were even stretch marks visible, ostensibly from two past pregnancies. What was even more amazing was that she was supposed to be pregnant even now, the result of the last lovemaking before her husband died in a terrible automobile accident just a month ago.

I took off my bra and slipped the panties down. The breasts were a little heavy, and the nipples were somewhat large. They sagged without the bra, supposedly the result of those two pregnancies, two nursing children, and age. What really amazed me was what I saw between my legs. Or rather, what I did not see between my legs. There was a nicely shaped patch of auburn hair. But there was no penis. There had been a penis there for nearly 42 years, but now I was that middle aged woman everyone else saw move in to the house on Sackett Street.

Chapter 1

I still could not believe what had happened to me over the past several months. Actually, it had been just over a year since I "disappeared" on that last mission. It was to be a particularly dangerous job and I had made some special arrangements beforehand. I was expecting to be a wanted man by the particular cartel after I accomplished my assignment, and I wanted to protect my family. I arranged for the service to pay my wife and family "insurance' money if I died or disappeared. I wanted to be sure that they were taken care of if I could not return. If the job went as I expected it would, I would have to disappear so they could not find me or be likely to bother my family.

The service arranged a very effective end to my prior life. In a very public place, and in a very public way, I "died" in a very routine car accident. My wife knew that I really did not die, but she did not know where I was going. She put on a very good show of grief at the funeral, some of which must have been real, as I was not likely to return any time soon. I promised her that I would ensure that she and the children were going to be taken care of and that I would keep an eye on them. Not a happy scene, but seemingly necessary.

After I disappeared, the subject of my new identity came up. The cartel was especially good at tracking folks like me down, and had in fact, killed two other officers in the past couple of years. After some discussion, I offered that it would be effective for me not only to change identity, but to change sex, too. Now, I must admit that my years of closet transvestism did lead me to think of that, but it actually did seem like a good idea to keep me alive.

I grew up in the Midwest. As early as age two or three, I vaguely remember putting my sister's blouses on and enjoying it. There were scattered occasions of cross-dressing throughout my life. When I was seven or eight, my sister and I would put on her dress-up clothes while we played in the basement, all clothes our mother had discarded. Later, as a teenager, I kept a private collection of clothing that I would wear whenever I found myself left home alone. I even took some with me to college, and would dress as a woman whenever I could find the time by myself.

Many times I would dream about becoming a woman, but had essentially proven to myself that I was only a transvestite, not really a transsexual, although the thought was extremely arousing to me. Later, after joining the service, I had occasional cross-dressing periods, all at home when my wife and family were away. My wife knew about it, and while she did not really condone it, and certainly would not participate, she allowed it.

To make the long story short, after the contrived accident, I entered a hospital under an assumed name. Following several months of hormone treatments, a lot of theatrical training, work on how to wear clothes and put on makeup, and finally, a lot of surgery, I emerged as Marcia Stephens. I was 43 years old, the widow of John Stephens who had recently been killed in an automobile accident, mother of two grown children, and pregnant with a third, conceived just before my "husband's" untimely death. I chose to move to the same town in which my wife lived, although she was unaware at the time. The service found me a nice three-bedroom house, and arranged the move.

The bit about being pregnant was the idea of one of the doctors at the hospital. After some concern over whether I would be accepted as female, should I make an inadvertent error somewhere along the line, we decided that to be pregnant would remove all doubt in anyone's mind. The doctors placed a balloon like object in my abdomen and would, over time slowly inject saline solution into it, gradually increasing its size over the course of the "pregnancy." My prenatal care appointments would ensure that it increased at an appropriate rate. Extra hormones would start my new breasts lactating at the correct time. All in all, a nice plan and one that amazed me.

I met the first of my neighbors a couple of days after I moved in from across the backyard fence. I had just taken the trash out to the alley and I heard her call to me.

"Hello, there," she said.

I looked up and saw a pretty blond woman looking over the fence, smiling.

"Hello," I was still unsure of my voice, although the operation on the vocal cords had raised the pitch somewhat.

"I'm Marcia."

"Hi, Marcia," she answered. "I'm Barbara. Barbara Thomas. I hope your move went okay."

"Just fine. Nothing broken or anything."

"That's good. Where did you move from?"

"Los Angeles," I kept to my new story line. Actually it was the truth, but some details were slightly modified.

"What brings you here?"

"Well," I launched into my story, "My husband was just killed in an auto accident, and I had to leave Los Angeles. Too expensive."

I could see here face sadden immediately.

"I'm so sorry. I shouldn't have asked."

"No, no. It's all right. The funeral was last month."

She was still standing there with a sad look on her face.

"Would you like to come over for a cup of tea?" I asked, smiling again.

"I would love that. Can I bring something?"

"Oh, no. That's not necessary."

"I have some crackers and some cheese. I'll get that and be right over."

I nodded and hurried inside to straighten the living room a bit. I was as nervous as I had ever been. Here I was, going to entertain a woman in my own house for the first time. I didn't know if I could do it. All the training had led to that event, but it was still the first time.

The room did not need much straightening, just a magazine or two out of place. I saw her walking up the sidewalk. I looked at myself in the mirror. I looked fine. I felt nervous, but I looked fine. The doorbell rang.

"Come on in, Barbara," I said as I opened the door.

"We'll go into the living room. I just put the teapot on. It will be a few minutes."

I was so nervous I was talking ninety miles a minute.

"Oh, you have such a beautiful home, Marcia. And so soon after you moved in. You must be exhausted."

"The movers did most of the work."

"Still, I had boxes all over the floor for weeks after I moved in."

"Here," I pointed to one of the chairs, "you can sit here."

We sat down and began chatting.

"So, Barbara, do you have a family?"

"Yes. I'm married...to Phil and have three children...Mary, she's twelve, Martin, he's ten, and Rebecca, she's two."

"Well, maybe I can get some of your baby things from you."

"Oh?" Barbara looked at me.

"I'm pregnant. I found out just after John died. I'm about six weeks along."

"Oh, that's wonderful!" Barbara was gleaming. "Of course you can have some of the baby things. Let's see, that means you're due in...April, right?"

"That's right. It's been so long since I was pregnant, it will almost be like the first time for me again."

"Oh, nonsense. Just like riding a bicycle."

She laughed and I just had to as well. Barbara was a wonderful person and would be a good neighbor.

"Are those your children?"

She was looking at two photos on the wall.

"Yes. That's William, he's 21, now, and the other is Maria, she's 19. They're both away at college."

"Such nice looking children. Aren't you excited about having another baby?"

"It's a bit late in life, but, yes, I am glad."

She got up and walked over to my wedding photo. She stood in front of it silent for several seconds.

"He was very handsome," she said.

"Yes," I agreed. It was funny, but I had actually only known that man for a couple of hours while we were taking the pictures. He was a nice looking man, and had been very friendly during the photo session.

"Your dress is so pretty," Barbara went on.

"I thought so. I haven't seen it for a long time."

"Do you have it wrapped?"

"At my sister's house. I didn't move it here."

"Very pretty."

She moved on down the hallway, looking at the other pictures. There was a formal portrait of me. I was wearing a red suit and a red and white hat. I looked very serious, but it was a good photo.

"This one is very recent, isn't it?" Barbara asked.

"Yes," I answered. "Only last April. The one of my husband was taken at the same time."

Next to mine was one of my "husband," also in a suit, and also looking very serious.

"We were so serious when we had those taken. I don't know what we were thinking."

"They are very good portraits. It looks exactly like you."

"Well, thank you."

"Maybe I'll come over and borrow that suit, some day."

"You'll have to gain too much weight for that, I'm afraid."

"Nonsense. I'm at least thirty pounds more than I should be."

"You are very kind," I said, laughing at the same time.

Barbara was a good three inches shorter than I was and a good thirty pounds lighter. I was a size 16 and she was more likely a 12. Still, she made me feel good.

I heard the teapot start to whistle in the kitchen.

"The hot water is ready. I'll go get the tea going," I said.

"I'll go with you."

We went into the kitchen, took the teapot from the stove, got down the tea bags and a pair of teacups. We sat at the breakfast table in the kitchen and made our tea.

"This is such a nice kitchen. It is so much more roomy than mine," Barbara said, looking around.

"It is nice. I've never had one this big. And only for one person, now."

"We'll have to use it for Thanksgiving and Christmas. I'm sure we can find enough people to make it crowded."

"That would be fun. I hardly ever really cook a meal. Maybe twice a week if I'm energetic."

"I'm sure you're a great cook," Barbara smiled at me and then took a sip of tea.

"I absolutely love Constant Comment," she said.

"So do I," I agreed. "Constant Comment tea and Orange Cappuccino coffee."

"You, too?"

"Me, too."

"I think I must buy three cans of Orange Cappuccino every time I go to the store."

"Sounds like me. I probably have that many cans in the cupboard right now."

We talked for hours and emptied the teapot twice. Barbara left well after dark with much laughter and cheerful conversation. I had a good friend. One who would stand with me for many years.

I had been up since seven that morning, and having worked at putting things away most of the day before Barbara came to visit, I was tired. I went to my bedroom and undressed. I pulled a cotton nightgown over my head, sat down at the vanity, and brushed out my hair. I looked at myself in the mirror. I was still looking at a middle-aged woman. She was just sitting there in a demure cotton nightgown, looking back at me. I was a better person, though. I had a friend, now, in that house on Sackett Street.

Chapter 2

Sunday was a beautiful day. I got up early and started to get ready to go to church. I had wanted to go for some time and this was the day. There were a number of reasons for going. One, it was the right thing to do. Two, I wanted to meet some people and make friends. And, three, I knew my wife was there and wanted to see her. She didn't know I was in the area and really had no idea about me. I didn't think I would actually go up and talk to her, but I did at least want see her.

I took off my nightgown and got into the shower. The warm water felt good as it ran down my shoulders and back. It felt great to soap up and caress myself. It made me feel so much better and ready to start the day.

I turned the shower off and stepped out. I quickly toweled off and then pulled my robe on. Slipping on my horseshoes, I went out into the kitchen to make a cup of coffee and some toast.

After the quick breakfast, I went back to my room to get dressed. I had decided the day before to wear a new suit. It had a black, slim skirt that came down to mid calf. The top was a blue tunic with gold buttons up the front. I would wear a white satin, high collared blouse under it. The waist was pulled in with a wide, black leather belt with a large gold buckle. I had a pair of thin, black leather gloves I would wear with the outfit.

I hung my robe up on the back of the bathroom door and went to my dresser. I opened my top drawer, took out a pair of light blue panties, and quickly pulled them on. I still wasn't used to not having to do something with a penis. It felt a bit strange to pull the panties on and have them fit so well.

I took a bra from the next drawer and put it on. It was of matching blue nylon lace and, for being so fancy, as well as being an underwire, was one of my more comfortable bras.

Next I got out a pair of black pantyhose and, sitting on the bed, pulled them on. Over all that I pulled on a slip, of the same blue lace as the bra and panties. As I often did, I looked at myself in the mirror, still amazed at the transformation. I then walked over to the closet.

First I took the blouse off the hanger and put it on. It was of white satin, with long sleeves and a high collar, buttoned up the back. The black skirt slipped on easily and I hooked it at the waist, tucking the blouse in carefully. I enjoyed

14

seeing the lace of my slip just barely visible through the translucent material of the blouse. Then, I took the blue tunic from the closet and slipped it on, buttoning the five gold front buttons. The tunic fit very well, having been tailored to hug my curves very closely without being tight. The high collar of the blouse rose above the round neckline. I buckled the black belt. My waist and hips were accentuated nicely.

The suit was very pretty, and I loved to see myself in it. It was at once professional, and attractive. I looked over at myself in the mirror and liked what I saw. I walked to the dresser and quickly brushed my hair out. After a little makeup, I put on a pair of simple pearl earrings and put a pearl pin above my left breast. I slipped on a dressy gold watch to compliment the gold buttons.

Going over to the closet, I picked out a pair of navy blue leather pumps. They had very high heels and I liked the way they make my legs look. I knew that my feet would be sore by the time I got home, but I would wear them anyway. I put on my gloves, picked up my purse, made sure I had my keys and billfold, and headed out the front door to my car.

The drive didn't take long, only about five minutes, but I enjoyed the trip. The sun was out, a warm breeze was already blowing, and I could smell flowers. I was happy, yet nervous about seeing Debbie. She had been out of my life for over a year. I wondered if she would recognize me for who I was. I was different, but was I enough different. I wanted her to recognize me, yet I was afraid she would.

I pulled into the driveway of Village Presbyterian Church and quickly parked. I got out, looked around a bit, and walked slowly to the front door. I could see many people around, from children to older folks. They were all smiling, and seemed to be friendly. I kept an eye out for my wife. I knew Debbie had started coming here after I disappeared. I walked in the front door of the sanctuary and was greeted by a pleasant middle-aged couple that shook my hand and handed me bulletin. I walked inside the sanctuary down the center aisle. It was a beautiful church, with lots of dark wood and colorful stained glass windows. I found a seat near the aisle and sat down. A young couple sat just down the pew from me with an older woman sat just beyond them.

The service was very nice and only took about an hour. I had looked for Debbie all through the service, but she evidently wasn't there. I could only hope she would come for second service and I was prepared to stay if that was what it took to see her. I had no intention of talking to her, but I just had to see her. I had to see if she was all right.

Once the service was over, the congregation went out onto the patio for coffee. It was all very friendly, with several people coming up to me and introducing themselves.

I chatted with the couple that sat in my pew, learning that they were newly married and just starting out life together. I met the minister briefly, who invited me to come back the next Sunday, and I met his wife, a very friendly woman, who I decided I wanted to get to know.

Then I saw her. Debbie was walking onto the patio. She was alone. She had apparently just arrived, probably intending to attend the second service. It was all I could do not to go over to talk to her. I hadn't seen her in nearly a year. I just stood there and watched her from a distance, drinking coffee and chatting with a woman who had just come up to see me.

"I'm so happy you decided to worship with us," the woman said. Her nametag said her name was Marian Tolliver. She was about 50 years old and very pleasant.

"I think I will enjoy coming here," I answered, stealing a glance toward Debbie. She was with a small group of two men and a woman, just talking.

"Well, I think so, too," Marian continued. "We have a wonderful choir and the women's circles are lots of fun and interesting."

"I saw the list in the bulletin," I said, trying to be attentive to her. "I see one or two I might check out."

"Please do," Marian was smiling. She saw me look over at Debbie.

"Do you know her," she asked me.

"She looks like someone I know."

"That's Debbie Watson. She lost her husband last year. Very active. Do you want me to introduce you?"

"No, thank you." I answered. "I'll go over myself in a little while."

"I have to go, now," Marian said. "Do come back."

"I will. I'll be here next Sunday."

I walked to the coffee table to refill my cup. I stirred in some cream and sugar and sipped as I watched Debbie. It was wrong for me to walk up to her, then, so I just drank my coffee and watched the people.

Finally, it was time to leave. The crowd had thinned out,

Debbie went into to church, and I was nearly alone. I started walking toward the parking lot to leave.

"I haven't seen you here before, have I."

It was a male voice from behind me. I turned and saw a graying, 50ish man wearing a very nice three-piece suit.

"No," I answered. "This is my first time here."

"Welcome to Village Church."

"Thank you. Everyone has been so very nice."

"We like to think so. I hope we will see you again."

"I am sure you will. I'm Marcia Stephens."

I held out my hand and he gently shook it.

"I'm Ed Tucker. Nice to meet you."

I shivered slightly as he held my hand. I looked at his eyes. They were friendly. His hand was gentle. He had a gentle look to him. I didn't know what to think.

"This is such a friendly church. I am so glad I decided to come."

"Very friendly," he answered. "Do you have a family here with you?"

"My children are all grown, and my husband died in July."

"Oh, I am sorry to hear that. My condolences."

He was genuinely sad for me. I could see it in his eyes.

He reached out and held my elbow as though to support me.

"Thank you," I said. "I have a home of my own not too far from here and I get along quite nicely, now."

"Very glad to hear that. Would you be interested in having breakfast after church sometime? We often get a group together after the first service and go to a little place just down the road."

"That sounds very nice. I'd like that."

"In fact, we have a group going this morning. Would you be interested?"

I was taken aback. I didn't know if I was ready for that, yet. A man showing interest in me.

"I think not today. Perhaps next Sunday."

"Next Sunday, then."

"Well," I said nervously. "I really should be getting home."

"I'll be looking for you next week."

"Thank you. I'll be here."

I turned and walked out to my car and got in. As I started the engine, I realized I was shaking. I was actually excited and nervous from having spoken to a man who seemed to like me. It was almost too much to experience. I started the car, pulled out and drove home.

Chapter 3

I was as excited as a teenaged girl. At least I think that's what it was like, not having had any teenaged girl experiences. But, it sure was exciting. I was going to a wonderful formal dinner party and I had a brand new dress to wear. It was specially purchased just he week before and fitted to me exactly. As I came from the shower I saw it hanging on the closet door. It was beautiful. The skirts were of dark green satin. The bodice was of an even darker shade of green velvet. It had a collar of green satin that outlined the low cut that would show the tops of my breasts to their best advantage. Around the waist was a green satin bow that sat at the small of my back. I just couldn't wait to get it on.

I reached into the top drawer and pulled out a pair of white lace panties. I slipped them up my legs and up around my bottom. They were pretty with lace all over the front. Then I took out a garter belt, also of white lace, pulled the straps through the panties, and then attached them to a lovely pair of dark stockings with a cute lace design in them. Next I put on the brassiere. It was white with the same lace as the panties and garter, and it pushed my breasts up into a nice cleavage that I knew would keep a lot of eyes busy that evening.

To pull my somewhat thick waist in, I then put on a sexy corset of white satin with lace overlay. After I laced it so tight that I could hardly breath, I had a figure I could die for. Then I put the petticoats on, two very full petticoats. I could hardly wait for the dress.

I walked over to the phone and dialed my neighbor's number. She picked up after only one ring.

"Barbara, I'm ready for you to help me with the dress."

"I'll be right there."

She was over in a few minutes. I opened the door for her.

"Oooh, I love the corset. You must be dying in there."

"True," I nodded, "but the men will love me for it."

"So true."

We went upstairs and into my bedroom where the dress was hanging. I slipped into a pair of heels and got ready to put the dress on.

"I just love your dress, Marcia."

"It is pretty, isn't it?"

"Very pretty. You'll be good enough to eat with that on."

She went to the closet and took the dress off the hanger. She opened the back zipper and held it out.

"Okay, are you ready?"

I walked over and held my arms out. I slipped my arms under the skirts and up into the top, then pulled it up over my head. My arms slipped into the sleeves and the dress fell down around me. It was quite heavy but felt good. Barbara zipped up the back and it fit perfectly. Then she worked on the back bow and then announced me dressed.

"You're perfect. Scrumptious."

"Help me with my hair a minute."

"Sure, it's just mussed a little. Where's that bow you wanted?"

I pointed to it on the dresser, and she quickly picked it up and pinned it to the back of my hair. I looked at myself in the mirror and shuddered. I was pretty. Not a svelte young thing, but I did look good. Good enough that a man would want to dance with me, perhaps. Good enough to want to have a romantic evening, perhaps. What about sex?

"What are you thinking, Marcia?"

"Oh, nothing," I lied.

"You were, too," she smiled. "You are very pretty and the men will want to be seen with you. Don't worry about it. Just smile a lot, laugh at their jokes and don't drink any alcohol."

"Good advice," I smiled back. Barbara was a good friend.

"When is your ride coming?"

"Oh, he's probably out there already. I'm late, as usual."

"Well, he'll be glad he waited."

Barbara smiled and headed out the door to check the front.

I looked at myself in the mirror once again. I was giddy with excitement. I was going to have a great time tonight, and I was going to have sex with a man. I knew it would happen. Ed was a nice man, I liked him a lot, and tonight was the night. We would go to the party, dance, and have a good time. He would take me out to eat, then some drinks and then I would invite him to spend the night with me. Just like that, and we would make mad passionate love all night long.

"He's here, Marcia," Barbara called.

"Okay, I'll be right there."

I walked out of the room and around the corner and there was Ed, dressed in a great looking black tuxedo. He was so handsome. He was holding my cape and had a big smile on his face. Ed and I had hit it off immediately after we first met. We couldn't wait to see each other at church each Sunday, and he often asked me out to breakfast or brunch after services. I had been nervous, but accepted and it began a great romance. It was really strange, since I still felt like I was married to Debbie, but since I wasn't really a man any more, I couldn't see worrying about that too much. Besides, he was so nice to me, I just couldn't say no.

Ed walked over and helped me put on my cape. Then, the sweet guy, he leaned over and kissed me. My knees nearly buckled, but I kissed him back and we headed out the door.

The evening was as expected. The party was great, with lots of friends, and fun dancing. I especially liked to slow dance with him. He was so smooth and I felt like he was softly carrying me across the dance floor. He would pull me close to him and I could feel him getting aroused. It was exciting thinking that I was causing his arousal.

Dinner was super. I ate as lightly as I could, but it was hard to turn down such wonderful food. It was all I could do but to look across the table at the wonderful man who was doting over me so romantically. He ordered wine, a nice burgundy, and we toasted each other several times.

After dinner came the real surprise. He drove me downtown and we got out in front of the Symphony Hall. The billboard hailed the Philharmonic Orchestra and billed a nice concert of Beethoven and Tchaikovsky. I was thrilled.

"Oh, Ed," I exclaimed. "This is wonderful."

"Just for you," he responded.

We entered in splendor, Ed escorting me on his arm, he in his handsome tuxedo, and me in my new gown. He showed the ushers the tickets and they led us to the greatest surprise of the evening. They showed me to my seat in a loge, overlooking the stage from the side of the hall.

"Ed," I was nearly speechless. "This is marvelous. A loge seat is just so romantic."

Ed smiled and helped me to sit down. He eased my cape off and laid it over the back of my chair. When he sat down next to me I reached over and took his hand. I looked into his eyes and realized that this man was truly amazing. He leaned over and kissed me lightly on the lips. I was beginning to melt inside.

The rest of the evening at the concert went like a blaze. The music was superlative, and I was falling head over in heels in love with Ed. During the intermission we went to the lobby where Ed introduced me to several of his acquaintances. He brought me a glass of wine and we tasted a few samples of cheese.

"Ed," I whispered to him as we walked back to our seats, "How on earth did you afford all this?"

"Hush, pretty lady," he said, in mock horror. "One does not ask such things of a gentleman."

"Pardon me," I blushed. "I love you for all this, though."

He stopped just before we got to the loge. He held me by the waist and kissed me gently.

"I love you, Marcia," he said. "I want only the best for the best woman in town."

I melted entirely. I leaned up and kissed him. I felt him hold on to me and pull me closer to him. His strong arms wrapped around and held me close, our hips pressing to each other, our mouths desperate for more of each other.

I don't remember any of the rest of the concert, except that it was beautiful and that I held his arm through it all, leaning on his shoulder. The evening was incredibly romantic. I had fallen hopelessly in love and had only eyes and ears for Ed.

Driving home, I leaned over and laid my head on his shoulder. He kept talking to me about how lovely I was and what a great evening he had. We drove to a park where we could look over the city. It was a pretty view. He parked the car and reached over to me. He leaned over and kissed me. It was wonderful feeling his tongue flick inside my mouth. I kissed him back. I slipped my hand to his thigh and felt his leg. His left hand came across and he held my waist. Then I felt him move his hand upward along my side. I kept kissing him, not daring to discourage any move he might make. His hand reached up under my right arm and then moved to my right breast. I moved so that it fell fully into his hand. He rubbed it through the material of my dress. I moaned slightly and moved my right hand further up along his thigh.

He pulled his hand away for a second, and then I felt his fingers touch the skin on the top of my breasts. Downward they crept and then inside my dress. He slipped his fingers further downward and then underneath my bra, just brushing the nipple on my right breast. I moved just slightly and he was able to slip his entire hand inside the cup of my bra, holding my breast. The feeling was wonderful.

My right hand moved further up his thigh, then landed on the most wonderful feeling hard spot. I had felt that hardness all evening and now wanted to get closer to it. He moved his hips as soon as I touched it. It was almost completely hard as it stretched against the material of his trousers. I rubbed the palm of my hand against it and I could feel it pulse. I wanted to see it. I wanted to taste it.

I reached over with my other hand and quickly unzipped his trousers. He moved his hips slightly to help and unhooked the waist gripper. I reached inside his white underpants and there it was. It was hot. It was wonderful. I pulled his underpants down and I saw his hard penis reaching up for me. I leaned down and kissed the tip.

"Oh, Marcia," he moaned.

The taste was a bit salty. I had never done that before. I had never believed I would actually be holding a man's penis in my hand and kissing it. I could feel the warmness starting to spread in my own abdomen, though, as I became excited at how I was obviously affecting this man. I had made this wonderful erection happen. It was me that made this man want to have me sexually. I could see that there was semen starting to come out the end. He was already wet. I opened my mouth and took the tip inside. He immediately pushed against me forcing a bit more in. He groaned. His hands began to hold my head and play with my hair. He leaned his head back. Taking it out of my mouth I licked the entire length, holding his testicles in my hand. Then, I put it back in my mouth and began sucking on it softly, moving my head up and down, up and down, slowly feeling the soft silky skin of his wonderfully hard penis slide past my lips and tongue.

Ed's hips began to move more quickly now. He arched his back and began pushing against me with his hips, raising his penis higher and higher, forcing more and more into my mouth. I kept licking and sucking, and then, with a loud groan, I felt a gush in the back of my throat.

"Oh, my God," was all he could say as he bucked against me. My mouth filled with a salty liquid. I let it drip from my mouth down along his penis and into his pubic hair. I kept licking until he reached down and held my head with his hands.

"Oh, stop, Marcia," he moaned. "I can't stand any more. You're so wonderful."

I sat back, knowing that my face must have been a fright, with his semen dripping from my mouth, but he leaned over and kissed me on the mouth. Kissed all that wonderful semen he had just given me. I wanted more of it, but I wanted it somewhere else. I wanted it somewhere else tonight.

"I love you so much, Marcia," he said, looking directly into my eyes.

"I love you, Ed. You are such a wonderful man to love me."

Then I said it.

"Ed," I spoke. I wasn't even nervous. "Spend the night with me."

I looked up at him.

He was silent for a second.

"Please, Ed. Spend the night with me. I want you to."

"I'd love to, Marcia."

I was happy.

We went into my house and he helped me take off my cape. I hung his jacket up in the front closet and watched him take off his tie.

"I know you love me in this dress," I said, "but I have to get out of what's holding me inside it. It's killing me."

"Can I watch?"

"I want you to watch. Come with me."

I took his hand and he followed me to my bedroom.

"Unzip me," I turned my back so he could reach the zipper of my gown. He carefully ran the zipper all the way to the bottom. He detached the large bow.

"What should I do with this?"

"Just lay it on the dresser."

I slipped the top of the dress off and let it fall from my arms. Then I let it fall from my hips and I stepped out of it. Ed just looked at me. I was standing in front of this gorgeous man in a corset, my breasts held out for him, with a sexy lace petticoat. I untied the petticoat and let it fall on top of the dress. He kept looking at me, now with just my lingerie between that wonderful man and me.

"Now, help me out of this corset. It's killing me."

I turned my back to him and felt his hands begin to untie the laces. It felt immediately wonderful when I loosened the laces and even better when it came free. I was now next to this sexy man in just my panties, brassiere, garter belt, and hose. My heels were still on, and somehow I thought he would think that sexy. I turned around to look at him. I leaned up against him, wrapping my arms around his neck and kissed him. He moved his hips against mine and I immediately felt the wonderful hardness of his erection against my belly. I wanted it so badly it was all I could do to keep from tearing his clothes off.

"Now lets get you undressed."

I didn't take long and he was naked in front of me with a wonderfully large erection. I moved my hand down, took hold of it, and heard him suck in his breath. I knew that feeling, but this time it was different. I wanted that hard thing inside me. I wanted to taste it then wanted it to push up inside me so I could be one with this wonderful human being who had been so kind to me. He didn't even care that my breasts were a little saggy, that my waist was a little thick, or that I had stretch marks. I thought he was wonderful.

He reached down and slipped his hand inside my panties. His fingers crept down between my legs, toward my private spot and then I felt it. I felt a feeling I had never before experienced. He moved his finger inside me, slipping up inside my vagina. I instinctively opened my legs and let him reach further in, letting him

25

slip his finger inside me. It felt so wonderful. I had never felt this before. I was glad I had moistened my vagina earlier in the evening.

His finger moved in and out ever so slowly and gently. I rubbed my hand over his penis and down under to cup his balls. He leaned down and kissed me. His tongue reached inside my mouth and my knees buckled. He slipped my panties slowly down my legs, running his hands along my bottom and along my thighs. I was trembling with excitement as I stepped out of them. He held me closer to him and I felt the warmness of his erect penis against my belly. I pushed against it as though to drive it directly into my belly where I wanted it so badly.

He held me and laid me on the bed. Ever so gently he lay down next to me and continued to rub his hands all over my body. He slipped a finger just inside my bra and rubbed it over my nipple.

"Take my bra off and lick my breasts"

He reached down quickly and before I knew it had unsnapped my bra and whisked it away. His mouth was full on my right nipple and I reveled in the feeling. My wife always said there was a direct connection between the nipples and the clitoris, and I now knew what she meant. My legs spread and I could feel my vagina opening. The vaginal jelly I had placed inside earlier was melting and running down between my legs. I was wetter than I could ever remember being before.

"Come inside me. Come inside me, now."

I was on my back, dressed only in my garters and stockings. My shoes were still on. I spread my legs, almost instinctively, and pulled at him.

Ed moved on top of me. I could feel a little of his weight, but he was careful. He slipped his penis in between my legs. The warmness of it thrilled me. The hardness of it excited me. I reached down and took hold of it and felt it pulse in my hand. It was almost like a separate living thing.

Carefully I moved my hips and with my hand I guided it into my vagina. I had never had a penis in there before. I had practiced with a dildo, but this was the first time with a man. It was so warm, almost hot. I loved it as it slipped inside so slowly. I could feel my insides filling up. I could feel a wonderful sensation just filling my belly as he moved his warm erection in and out slowly. I reached up and pulled him down to me to kiss him. I pulled him against me as he began moving faster and faster. I could feel his testicles tickling my bottom. I could feel his penis reach deep inside me then pull almost all the way out. His breathing was getting shorter and shorter and he was moving faster and faster. Suddenly he held his breath and pushed in as far as he could.

"Oh, I love that," I said.

I spread my legs as far as they could go, then wrapped them around him. I wanted to hold him to me as tightly as I could. I felt the heels of my shoes touching his back. I squeezed as tightly as I could, feeling his wonderful hard penis pushing in and out of me.

"Oh, Marcia."

He pushed even harder and, with a shudder, I felt a warm gush between my legs as he came inside me. He gave me his wonderful seed. His wonderful seed with which I could do nothing, but I accepted it as a sign of his love for me. I was now a real woman being loved by a real man. I hugged him tightly to me.

He moved slightly, starting to pull out, but I held him in. I wanted to keep feeling him inside.

"I want to do you," he murmured softly.

"Just stay inside me," I answered. "I love that feeling."

He kissed me and kissed me again. His hand reached down between us. I could feel his fingers reach my pubic hair. I moved slightly and his hand reached down between us and touched my clitoris. I reacted like touched by fire. I kissed him madly and pushed my hips up against him. It felt so good. He moved sideways, pulling out, and ran his hand down fully between my legs. His finger slipped inside then quickly back out to rub softly against my clitoris. I arched my back and moved my hips up, pressing my pubis against his hand. I was coming and suddenly I felt it all release. It spread all through my belly and outward like a warm rush. I strained every muscle and then relaxed them all. I grabbed his head and kissed him hard on the mouth. I had masturbated before, but never had I felt such a wonderful feeling, climaxing as a woman. Climaxing with a man making me come. I wanted him inside me again.

I frantically reached down to find his penis. It was still hard. I pulled him, urging him to move on top of me again. He slid over quickly and that wonderful hard penis slipped inside once again. I was complete again. I was so happy. I could feel tears and I began to cry. I just lay there as he moved his hips slowly, just barely moving his manhood in and out, in and out, just making me feel wonderfully fulfilled. We fell asleep.

I woke up the next morning and reached over to find Ed still asleep. I slid my hand along his belly until I found his penis. He had a wonderfully hard erection. I couldn't resist, so I carefully sat up, slid over on top of him, holding his penis in my hand, and slowly sat down on him. I was still very wet inside, with two loads of his semen still inside me.

With one finger I separated my labia lips, and then, nearly taking my breath away, I slid that wonderful hardness inside my open vagina. I sat down all the way, driving him as far into my belly as I could make it go. I rocked my hips and felt my clitoris rub him slightly. A shiver went completely through me and I let out an involuntary moan.

He groaned slightly and then opened his eyes. He smiled and pulled me down to him, licking my breasts as he lifted his hips to drive himself deeper into me. The feeling was absolutely wonderful. I felt so full and fulfilled at the same time. I moved my hips and slid up and down, up and down along his hard penis.

He kept kissing my breasts and held me close. He began pushing harder and harder. He nearly lifted me completely off the bed with his hips and he drove his penis deeper and deeper inside my very willing vagina. I was hot, and wet and wanted more. I could feel him tensing, and then with a loud groan, he pushed hard one last time with his powerful hips and came inside me. I could feel the warm moisture spreading inside. I leaned forward and kissed him, driving my tongue deep inside his mouth. He held me close. I felt his penis still inside me and I kept rocking my hips, back and forth. I could feel my clitoris rubbing on him and I was getting higher and higher. I couldn't believe the control I had over the situation and I just kept moving, nearly in automatic, not able to stop.

Ed ground his hips up at me, answering every move I made, and then I felt the uphill climb grow steeper and steeper. I closed my eyes and felt my climax coming. I pushed one last time and with a loud cry fell over the top with a magnificent orgasm. I had never felt like I did just then. I was exhausted, yet exhilarated. I wanted more, yet I couldn't go on. I thrashed for several seconds, driving my mouth onto Ed's and whimpering out of control. Finally I fell exhausted onto Ed's chest. As Ed ran his hands over my body, rubbing my back and my bottom, we fell back to sleep, together.

Chapter 4

I was nervous as hell. The day had been planned for weeks and it wasn't supposed to be a surprise for anyone. But I knew it would be hard. Hard for me. Hard for my wife.

Or was it ex-wife. We hadn't divorced, but as far as the world was concerned, I was dead and she was a widow.

The service had arranged the meeting. They had approached her after I had insisted, and they had told her everything. She had not taken it well, but was really glad I was still alive and well. She wasn't too sure about the sex change thing, though.

The meeting was arranged to take place in a park in a city near where we both lived. At that time, she did not know that I was living in the same town as she. I would tell her today. I got out of the car and closed the door. It was a bit chilly. I was wearing a grey wool skirt, white cotton blouse, and a long, red, cardigan sweater. I didn't want to dress up too much. Be too feminine. I just wanted to look comfortable and very normal. I decided to wear a pair of grey leather low heels, not too flashy. My hair was getting long, but I had pulled it back with a black bow. I wore a simple set of pearl earrings and a matching pearl necklace.

The park was not much more than a city square. There were lots of trees, old cottonwoods that spread out and shaded the ground from the summer sun. The grass was still a little green, but was starting to brown slightly around the edges of the sidewalks.

I saw her standing next to the water fountain that had been identified as the meeting place. I walked slowly toward her. I recognized her immediately. She was wearing her hair exactly as I had remembered. She wore the blue trousers I remembered, and the white blouse with the lace around the neck. I could hardly continue, but something drew me onward.

She turned around when she heard my footsteps and looked at me. I could see a look of amazement on her face, and then a look of fear. Then she went blank and just stared at me. I continued to walk up to her. She just stood there.

"Debbie?" I said softly.

"Mark?" she spoke tentatively.

"Yes," I nodded. "Except now it's Marcia."

"Marcia?"

I nodded. We were standing about six feet away from each other. Each of us had our purses clutched in front of us, just staring at each other. I was so nervous my knees were shaking. I was glad I wasn't in a pair of really high heels.

"You have been going to Village Church, haven't you?" Debbie asked.

"Yes," I answered. "For quite some time, now."

"They told me a little about all this."

"I know that," I answered. "I told them to. They didn't want to, but I insisted."

She just nodded.

"Can we sit down, Debbie. It might be better."

She didn't say anything, but we moved to a park bench not too far away. I sat at one end, she at the other. We were still on guard with each other. We nervously held our purses on our laps with both hands.

"How much did they tell you?"

"They told me about the car accident. And they told me about the operations. And they told me about the plan to keep you undercover."

"That's pretty much it. Did they tell you where I'm living, now?"

"No," she shook her head.

"Just a few blocks away from you. On Sackett Street."

She just looked at me.

"I don't know whether to me happy or angry," Debbie said.

"You know that I would be dead if I didn't do this."

"That's what they told me. But that doesn't change my feelings."

"I still love you. And I have missed you a lot."

"Don't say that," she was almost angry, and she turned away.

"Okay," I went on. "but it's true. I made sure everything was taken care of. Is everything okay, now?"

"Oh, yes," she was crying now, "All that stuff is just fine. Nice house. Lot's of insurance money. But you aren't there, and you should be."

"We can still be together."

"How?"

"I'm here. We can still be together."

"But you...you aren't Mark any more."

"But I still know all our secrets and you know all mine. We still have a lot of good memories. And we could have more."

"What, as girlfriends?"

"Or sisters, or whatever."

"But I want a lover."

"We can do that, too."

"Oh, get real."

"Okay, but it's true. You know it's really me, despite what you see on the outside."

"Well, I need some time, Mark...or Marcia, whatever."

"Okay," I nodded, and stood up. "Do you want my phone number?"

She nodded her head. She was still crying.

I pulled out a small card and handed it to her. It had my new name, address, and phone number on it.

"Is it safe for me to know this?"

"I think so. They stopped looking for me a while back."

She just looked at the card.

"Marcia Lynn Stephens," she read from the card. "Mrs. Marcia Lynn Stephens?"

"That's the story line. I'm supposed to be a widow."

"Oh that's funny. You and me, too."

"See," I tried to smile. "More things in common."

She smiled, but still had not stopped crying. She stood up.

"Will you be in church Sunday?" Debbie asked.

"Yes."

"Does anyone else know anything about all this?"

"No one except the government people who are handling the case."

"No one at church?"

"No," I assured her. "No one at church."

"I'll see you at church, then."

"Okay," I answered. "I'll see you between services."

She nodded, still looking at me.

"You pick nice clothes," she said.

"Thank you," I responded, a little surprised. I did not know how to answer.

"I'll call you in a day or two after I've thought this over some more. I will call. Don't worry."

"Okay."

She turned and walked away. I watched until she got into her car. As she drove away I thought about all the years we had lived together. Lived together as husband and wife. Then I walked back down the sidewalk thinking how different things were. The click of my heels on the pavement, the swish of my skirt, the bounce of my breasts all serving to point out how very much different things really were.

Chapter 5

Debbie did call me. It was two days later. I was at home, working on paying bills, and the phone rang.

"Hello," I said.

"Mark?"

"Debbie?"

"Yes," she answered. "I just can't bring myself to call you Marcia, yet, I guess."

"That's alright," I said. "Just between you and me."

"Can we meet again?"

"Yes. I'd like that."

"How about now. Before I chicken out."

"Alright. Where?"

"I'll come to your house. Is that alright?"

"Yes, of course," I said. "Come on over. I wasn't doing anything important."

"Then I'll be over in about an hour."

We hung up and I my heart started fluttering. I was suddenly nervous, again. I looked around the house. It was neat. It never got messed up. Just a few magazines to pick up. A few minutes to clean up the bathroom.

I went to my room to make sure it was straight. I made the bed quickly and put a few scattered clothes away. I saw myself in the mirror. There she was again. That middle aged woman I saw every morning, looking back. What did Debbie see? I saw that I needed to brush my hair a bit, and to touch my makeup a little. I was wearing slacks and a white cotton blouse. Nothing fancy. Probably best that way.

The door bell rang almost exactly an hour after Debbie called me. I went to the door and opened it.

There she was, my wife, and she was beautiful. She was wearing a lovely red dress with a black leather belt and black patent leather heels. She was absolutely gorgeous. I was stunned.

"Oh, Debbie," I stammered. "You look wonderful. Come in."

She walked in without saying a word, just looking around.

"I should have put something else on," I said.

"Oh, you're just fine, Marcia. There I said your name."

What was going on?

"You have a lovely home."

"Thank you. Please sit down. Can I get you something to drink?"

"Just water, thank you."

She sat down on the couch, neatly crossing her legs, setting her purse on the couch next to her. I quickly grabbed two glasses and filled them with ice water from the refrigerator. I put the glasses down on the coffee table, then sat on a chair facing Debbie.

"I'm glad you decided to call me," I said.

"I wanted to get to know you, again," Debbie was actually smiling.

"Well, here I am. What you see is what you get."

"Oh, I doubt that, Marcia."

"Well, I guess you're right about that."

She smiled, picked up the glass of water, and took a sip. I noticed her lipstick was especially bright. A smear of red was left on the edge of the glass.

"So, Marcia," Debbie sat back on the couch. "Tell me about yourself. Tell me about your new life as a woman."

"Hmm," I started slowly. "The operations were over about two months ago and they moved me in here. I've been keeping the house and writing stories."

"Still writing?"

"Still writing."

"Do you like being female?"

"I don't have any choice, now. But, yes, I like it. I get along quite nicely. People treat me well."

"This is kind of right down your old line, isn't it?"

"You mean the cross dressing?"

"Yes. It sort of fits right in."

"That's true. That came to mind when we were looking for a way for me to hide from the cartel. They had found and killed the last four agents who were hidden. So far, they haven't gotten close, and I understand they have given up. They think I'm dead."

"You seem to keep the same kind of clothes you did before. A bit conservative."

"Yes, but being a 40 something widow didn't seem to call for anything else."

"A widow. Did they do up a full story on you...family, husband, children, everything?"

"Yes," I nodded. "See the pictures on the wall."

She stood up and walked over to the wall where the "family" photos were hanging. She saw the young man who was my "son", the young woman who was my "daughter" and a photo of me with a handsome man, my "husband."

"Nice looking family," she said. "What happened to your husband?"

"Car accident. Sound familiar?"

She nodded, then walked further down the hall to look at the rest of the pictures. She stopped in front of the wedding photo.

"Is this you?"

"They can do miracles with makeup, can't they. Made me look like I was twenty."

"Beautiful dress. Did they let you keep it?"

"No. That went back to the store. Too hard to explain a brand new dress that's supposed to be over twenty years old."

"I suppose," she turned back to me.

"I never saw you dressed as a woman before," Debbie said. "I didn't think I wanted to."

"The counselor didn't think it was a good idea."

"It probably wasn't then," Debbie was looking at the photograph of me with my "husband" and "children". "But you look so...normal...you know. Not at all like I thought."

"I want to look normal."

"Oh, you know," she looked at me for a second. "all those books of the transvestites looking like prostitutes or dressed up like little girls."

"I've never been like that."

"Some are."

I nodded.

"Of course," she went on, "I saw the kind of clothes you always kept in the closet. Nice things."

"You commented on that when I first showed them to you."

"Mark...Marcia," she was stammering, now.

I just turned toward her. I said nothing.

"Marcia," she had regained her composure, again. "I need to know something. It will be hard for me to hear it. It will probably be hard for you to say it, but I have to know. I promise that I will not get angry, or leave, but I have to know. I think I know the answer."

"Alright, Debbie," I said softly.

"Are you a complete woman? I mean, did they do everything to you?"

"I've had complete sex reassignment surgery, yes."

"So, you don't have a penis anymore?"

"No."

"And you have a vagina?"

"Yes."

"Have you...have you ever...uh...had sex with a man?"

I didn't answer right away, but I could see that she already knew the answer.

"Yes," I nodded. "I have been going out with a very nice man I met at church."

"And you have been making love?"

"Once we did."

She turned away from me for a second. She looked up at the ceiling and took a deep breath. Then, she turned back around.

"Is it possible that we could get back together?" she said, looking me in the eye.

"Of course we can get back together. You're here right now."

"No," she shook her head quickly. "I mean that I have missed you. I want to have sex with you. I miss being together with you."

"But I don't have a penis anymore."

"You told me that. I want to feel you against me again. I want to kiss you again, and I want to feel your hands against me again. That won't have changed."

I just stood there for a second. Then I reached my hands out and took hers. Her hands felt so good. Just like I remembered. Then we moved together and we hugged closely. Even that felt the same as old times.

"Oh, this feels good," Debbie said.

"Yes, it does," I responded. I couldn't believe how good it felt.

"Does this make us lesbians?" she asked.

"Who knows? Who cares?"

I leaned over and kissed her. She tasted just as I remembered. She responded just as I remembered. It was wonderful. Her hands went up my back just like she always did, and I moved my hands along her sides and up to touch the sides of her breasts. She moved to allow me to fully hold her breast and she kissed me deeper.

"Oh, Mark," she had her eyes closed. "It's been too long. Just like after one of those long deployments."

"You are wonderful. You are beautiful."

"You're not half bad yourself," she moved back from me a little and looked at me.

I took her hand and led her down the hall.

"Come on. Let me show you the rest of my house."

We walked down the hall and I showed her the dining room, the kitchen, the front room. Then I showed her my office and the spare bedroom. Then, a bit nervous, I showed her my bedroom. She walked in and looked around.

"Very nice. Nice furniture."

She walked over to my closet and looked in. The door was open and she could easily see what was hanging. She reached in and moved a few things around, obviously curious as to what was in the closet.

"I'll be glad to show you everything in there."

"Oh, I'm sorry," she pulled her hand back quickly. She was blushing.

"It's alright," I said as I walked over to her. "Here, I have lots of nice things. Dresses, skirts, blouses, slacks."

"Nice. Did they buy them for you?"

"Some of them. The rest I got myself."

"You do have good taste."

"I hope so," I said, holding a blouse in my hand as she touched it. It was my favorite blouse. White, sheer nylon with a lace collar and lace cuffs.

"It's so pretty," Debbie said. "I don't have anything that pretty."

"I know that's not true, Debbie."

"Well," she smiled back at me. "Maybe I do have something that pretty."

"And your dresses," she was looking in the closet again.

"So many. And evening gowns, too?"

"They are pretty, aren't they?"

"They are gorgeous. Do you get to wear them anywhere?"

"Ed took me to the symphony."

"I bet you were beautiful."

"Ed thought so."

"Is that the night you first made love?"

I did not answer immediately. She caught me by surprise with that question.

"Yes, Debbie," I finally told her. "We did make love that night."

She stopped and just gazed at the clothes in the closet. Then she turned and looked at me. She looked at my face, my body and my feet.

"I just can't believe it's really you."

"It's really me."

"Let me see you. Let me see what you really look like without the clothes."

"Right now?"

"Right now."

"Okay," I smiled. "Does this mean I get to watch you undress, too?"

She smiled.

"You always used to say that."

"True," I smiled, too. "See, I'm still in here, somewhere."

I started unbuttoning my blouse. Debbie was watching carefully. I pulled the shirttails out and then slipped it off. I was wearing a simple bra, but it was obvious that the breasts inside them were very real. I then unbuttoned my slacks and slipped them down, kicking my shoes off in the process. I was wearing pantyhose over a pair of panties. She could see that my hips were wider than before, and that I had a waist, although certainly not as thin as hers.

"Your turn," I said. "I'll show you mine if you show me yours."

"Very funny," she laughed, although I could see it was still hard for her. "You have bigger breasts than I do."

"I'm a bigger woman than you."

She nodded, then unbuckled her belt, dropping in on a chair. Then she began unbuttoning the gold buttons that ran the front of her dress. As she stepped out of it, I saw the pretty underwear. It was pink, and very lacy. She always liked to wear that sort of thing when she dressed up. She was standing in front of me in her slip.

I leaned over and started to roll my pantyhose down. I quickly got them off and tossed them onto the dresser. Now I was only wearing my bra and panties.

"Not as fancy underwear as you have. I didn't know you were going to dress up. I have nicer underthings."

"I wanted you to remember me as something sexy."

"I remember you as something sexy, alright."

"Take your bra and panties off. I want to see all of you."

I quickly unhooked the front clasp of the bra and then slipped the panties down. My breasts fell down, shaking slightly. I stood naked in front of my wife, goose bumps starting to form on my arms and legs.

"You really did have the operation, didn't you."

"Yes," I started to walk toward her. "What you see is what you get."

She just stood and stared at me for a few moments. Then she walked over toward me.

"Can I touch you?"

"Touch me."

She reached out tentatively with her hand toward my breasts, and touched the sides. She held it carefully and then lifted it slightly.

"Implants?"

"Yes."

"They look nice."

"Thank you."

Then she ran her hand down my front and touched my pubic hair.

"Your hair feels the same."

"That doesn't change."

She just stood there, looking at me.

"Here," I said. "I'll sit on the bed, and you can look me all over."

I sat down and spread my legs a bit. She could see my crotch. She could see my labia. She could see that there was definitely no penis there.

"This is strange," Debbie said. "I know it's you, but what I see is something else."

"Take your clothes off. When you feel me, you'll remember everything."

She pulled her slip up over her head, then dropped it on the floor. Then she took her panty hose off along with her panties. Then, with a quick flip of the wrist, her bra came off and I was looking at the woman who was my wife for twenty years. I remembered everything. I was remembering how I would get a wonderful erection watching her do that before.

Now, I just got a wonderful tingling sensation in my groin. I needed to put some moisture into my vagina before we went any further.

"There's one thing I need to do before we go any further. I don't get wet automatically. I need to help it along."

I leaned back on the bed and reached over to the bedside stand. I took out a tube of KY jelly.

"Do you want to do the honors?" I held it out to Debbie.

She took the tube from me and put some jelly on her finger. She came forward and slowly reached her hand down between my legs. She carefully placed her finger on the lips of my labia and worked the moisture into the folds. I jumped when she touched me. The jelly was a little cold, but I warmed it immediately. She kept moving her finger and soon it began to slip inside my vagina. I leaned back, closing my eyes.

"Does that feel good?" Debbie asked.

"Oh, yes."

"Let me put some more jelly in there."

She put some more on her finger and then put her finger deep inside my vagina. The feeling was wonderful. I was loving every sensation. She slipped her finger in and out and then brushed my clitoris. I jumped.

"Do you have a clitoris, too?"

"Oh, yes, I do."

"How did they do that?"

"It's part of my penis."

"Oh," she looked closer at it. "That's neat. Now I know where to look for your penis."

I smiled, and just let her run her fingers around my vagina and clitoris. I was warming up nicely.

Debbie climbed onto the bed and lay down next to me. I leaned over and kissed her. We kissed deeply and ran our hands over each other's bodies. I felt her breasts and ran my fingers down between her legs. I slipped my finger inside her

vagina and it was already soaking wet. She was obviously hot.

"How do we do this?" she said.

"Just like we used to do, except no intercourse."

"I'll miss that."

"I'll miss it, too."

"Go down on me."

I turned and moved my mouth to her love nest. She moved to mine and as I kissed her softly and put my tongue on her clitoris, she did the same for me.

"Oh, Debbie, I had no idea how good that was for you."

"It is good."

"Oh, keep doing that. Don't stop."

We licked and kissed and kept going. I was already high and kept going higher. I felt it reaching the limit.

"Oh, Debbie...."

I fell over the top in a crashing climax. I had never felt it before like that. It spread all through my tummy and I began to cry. I launched harder into making Debbie come.

She began tensing as soon as I came, and within seconds she tensed, and groaned and began thrashing. She reached down and made me stop licking her. I turned back and kissed her long and hard on the mouth. We held each other and caressed

for several long minutes.

"Does your new friend do that for you?"

"Ed?", I answered. "He hasn't done that. He did me with his finger."

"Did you like making love to Ed?"

"Yes," I answered, not sure where her questioning was going.

"Was it good?"

"It was good."

"Did you like having a penis inside you?"

"It was wonderful. Now I know why you loved it so much. I can't do that for you now."

"I know. I'm glad you can have sex with a man, though."

"Have you had sex since I left?"

"Yes," she answered. "Right after the funeral, I was really depressed. I had a friend from work and we went out a lot."

"Is he good?"

Debbie smiled.

"Yes, he's good."

"Do you still go with him?"

"Yes, I do. Does that bother you?"

"Probably just like it bothers you that I made love with Ed."

"Yes, I suppose you're right," she said. "Where did you say you met Ed?"

"At church."

"Now, describe Ed to me."

"Very tall, gray, 50ish, widower. Usually wears a three-piece suit to church. He sometimes ushers."

"I think I know who you are talking about. He is a good looking man."

"I think so. Are you jealous?"

"I should be. But I'm happy for you. Are you serious with him?"

"Oh, it's too early to tell. He doesn't know anything about my real past."

She leaned over and kissed my left nipple.

"I hope you are happy. I want you to be happy," Debbie said to me.

"Are you happy?"

"Yes," she sat up in bed." Actually I am. The kids are doing fine and Bill is wonderful to me."

"Bill? Is that his name?"

"Yes. Very nice to me. Wonderful in bed."

"As good as I was?"

"As good as you were," she laughed. "Well, maybe not that good. After all, you had twenty years to figure me out."

"Kiss me, again," I said.

She leaned over and we kissed.

"It's wonderful to taste you again," I said.

"Yes, it is."

"We'll have to be careful or we'll be the lesbians of the town."

"I won't tell if you won't."

"Deal, Debbie."

"Deal, Marcia," Debbie agreed. "Now, you do me."

Chapter 6

Ed picked me up just before ten that morning. We were going to have a picnic at the lake and I had put together a nice basket of food and a bottle of wine. It was going to be romantic and I wanted to be sure everything was ready. A bottle of Rosé wine, cheese, bread. Even flowers for the blanket. I wanted everything to be perfect. The weather was even perfect. I had it all planned.

I wore a simple loose fitting skirt and a thin, gauze cotton blouse. Underneath I wore only a pair of panties and a bra. I didn't want the extra encumbrances of pantyhose getting in the way. If Ed wanted to touch me, I wanted him to be able to reach all of me easily.

It really was perfect picnic. We had chosen a small hill overlooking the lake. A light breeze was blowing just enough to cool the heat of the sun. The tree provided just enough shade to keep us from burning.

We spread the blanket out on the grass beneath the tree. I looked out over the view of the lake below us as Ed opened the picnic basket and laid out the food and wine. I watched him uncork the wine and pour each of us a glass.

"To us," he said.

"To us," I responded, drinking a sip of the fine rose. I looked over at Ed. He was looking back at me. I knew what would happen. We wouldn't get very far into the lunch. He had those eyes that told me he wanted me for lunch. That was okay with me, as I had prepared for that eventuality. I could already feel the jelly in my vagina beginning to melt.

I reached over and touched Ed's leg. I ran my hand up his leg and rubbed his crotch, willing his erection to grow. He reached back and touched my breasts, rubbing them through the soft cotton of my blouse.

Ed was kissing me almost before I knew it, his hand running up under my skirt. I felt him run his tongue deep into my mouth the way I loved. The roof of my mouth was alive. My whole body was alive. His hand was sliding up my thigh and his fingers touched me through my panties. I moved my hips involuntarily, pushing toward his hand, wanting him to do more. I had purposely worn a pair of loose fitting cotton panties. They were cooler to wear than a pair of tight fitting ones, but especially they made it easier for Ed to get his hand inside when we started petting.

His finger slipped past the elastic of the leg opening and I felt it touch the lips of my vagina. I was already hot, and that was making me hotter. I kissed him harder and placed my hand on his lap, feeling the growing erection under his pants. I rubbed the palm of my hand urgently feeling his penis grow larger and larger.

His finger slipped inside me and I moaned out loud. I felt him slide it all the way inside me. I felt him touch the top of my vagina. I felt him touch all the way inside me, like he was reaching into my very soul.

My hands tore at his belt and his zipper. I nearly ripped his pants open and grabbed at his penis, desperate for the man. I kneaded his large, hard manhood through the fabric of his under shorts. Then, I drove my hands, both of them, inside and grabbed his wonderfully hard erection. With both hands I pumped him up and down. As his finger worked miracles inside me, I worked a miracle on his penis.

He was breathing in shorter and shorter breaths. He was nearly out of control, kissing me harder and harder. He slipped two fingers inside me with one hand, then pushed his other hand up underneath my blouse, cupping my breast.

With a quick motion, he pushed my bra up over my breast and his hand was full on my nipple. The next thing I knew he pushed me over onto my back and his mouth devoured my breast, his tongue licking my hardening nipple, driving even more fire into my burning insides.

"Ed," I said, breathlessly, "Ed, I want you, now."

Ed said nothing. He pushed me back and moved over me. He slipped his legs between mine and I felt his weight on my body. Then, with hardly any effort, he moved the opening of my panties aside and I felt the tip of his penis slip inside me. I felt it open me up wide and felt its heat melt me completely.

"Oh, my God," was all I could say as he came with a massive, loud groan. He was really worked up. He hardly lasted ten seconds inside me. It was wonderful to feel the spreading wetness between my legs.

He continued to pump for several seconds after he came, but finally he quit. He pushed up with his hands and looked down at me.

"Marcia," he said, smiling, a dreamy look on his face.

"I don't think I've come that fast since I was a kid."

"Oh?" I smiled back. "How many girls did you make love to when you were a little kid?"

"One or two," he said. "You really know how to get me worked up."

"I try," I said.

"I've never made love outdoors before."

"Neither have I."

"Did anyone see us?"

"Who knows?" I answered. "But, if they did, they got a good show."

We laughed. Ed rolled over, reluctantly pulling his very wet penis out of my now very wet vagina. I needed more.

"Ed," I said. "Don't forget me. I haven't come and I want to come louder than I ever have before."

"You mean you want me to do more of this?" he said as he touched my clitoris.

I closed my eyes as he pulled my panties off and his fingers grazed my now very sensitive clitoris. My legs opened wide and he slipped his finger inside once more.

Then, moving carefully, but quickly, he touched his tongue between my legs and I let out a cry.

He dove in fully as I held his head between my thighs. I felt him as he lashed his tongue against my clitoris, against my labia, against the inside of my thighs. I was going crazy with lust.

My hips were out of control as he continued to work my womanhood with masterful fingers and an even more masterful tongue. I could feel the tension rising and I felt the now ever more familiar rush building in my head. As I held onto his

head, nearly crushing him with my thighs and hands, I fell over the edge, shouting loudly, screaming into the outdoors, as he pushed me over the edge into a wonderful, crashing, long, climax.

I was desperate for more. I clawed at him and pushed him back. I pushed him onto his back, pulling his pants down just enough to get hold of his partially hard penis. I drove my mouth down over it, taking it in as far as I could. I could feel

it growing in my mouth. It excited me to feel it change from a soft piece of flesh into a hard, sexual piston. It excited me to know that it was I that was causing it to happen.

When it was as hard as I could ever remember it, I crossed my leg over him and sat down on him. I slid that huge erection up inside me, ramming my bottom down as hard as I could, wanting to force that manhood as far into my body as it would go. Ed groaned loudly. I moaned a long wail, my head thrown back.

We both came within a few seconds. I collapsed on top of him. Several minutes later I sat up. I looked down. Ed was laying back, just looking up at me. I was astraddle him, his penis still inside me, although soft. My skirt was spread out over us, covering his lap and hiding our sexual union. I laughed out loud.

"What's so funny?" Ed asked.

"Just look," I said. "Here I am sitting on you like we're just playing around. Those people over there are watching."

"What?"

"Don't worry, silly," I said. "They just walked up. They didn't see a thing. Now don't move or they'll see you don't have your pants all the way up."

I wiggled a little and gave his penis a squeeze with my vagina muscles. I felt him give me a little push and I smiled. I just moved my hips ever so slowly, not enough for anyone to see what was going on, but enough to make him get hard again. I had never felt a penis grow inside me. It was wonderful. It felt it fill me up in a way so much different than when he entered me. It filled me up everywhere at the same time. Ed closed his eyes, concentrating on not making any sounds and not moving in any obvious way. I just flexed my muscles, gripping around his growing erection.

I felt him growing more and more tense as he resisted moving. His penis was completely erect and I felt him flex it inside me. He was moving his hips just slightly, and I answered his movements with little ones of my own. I licked my lips so he could see my tongue. I looked into his eyes. He moaned just slightly.

I looked around and saw the people walking along the path just below us. It was a couple, just talking as they strolled along. The man looked up at us and waved, smiling. He resumed talking to the woman. The woman glanced up and looked at me. She took a double take. I smiled at her and she smiled back. I saw her hand reach around the backside of the man as she hugged him closer to her.

Just then Ed let out a huge moan and I felt him come into me. I didn't think a man could come that many times so soon, but he did. He thrust up into me and filled me again with his wonderful seed. I just rocked my hips back and forth, willing him to keep coming and keep filling me with his semen and that wonderful penis that I had come to love so much. The woman below looked at me one more time. She raised her hand behind the man's back and waved at me, giving me the okay sign with her thumb and forefinger. I smiled back.

Chapter 7

Debbie walked up to me in church one day. It was after the service and we were all out on the patio having coffee. I saw her coming toward me. She was wearing a blue tunic suit that fit her to a tee. She always looked so good when she wore clothes like that. I noticed she was wearing her navy blue pumps, the ones with the really high heels. She only wore those when she wanted to show off to a man.

"Hi, Debbie," I said with a big smile. I hadn't seen her for some days.

"Hi, Marcia," she was smiling too. "Your dress is beautiful. Is it new?"

I was wearing a spring print dress with a wide self-fabric belt. I had bought it the previous week and had only worn it once before, to a get together in the neighborhood. I really liked it and always wore my prettiest underthings with it. I

had on a pair of white, high heeled sandals.

"First time to wear it here," I answered. "I love your suit. You look so good in a suit."

"So do you, Marcia," she grinned at me. "Want to trade clothes?"

"What on earth is the matter with you?"

"Oh, nothing," she laughed. "Can we step over to the sidewalk for a second?" Debbie was suddenly serious.

"I have a personal question," she continued.

We walked over out of the way of the crowd. She leaned up close.

"Someone told me you were pregnant."

"Really?" I smiled. "Who said that?"

"Shawna."

Shawna was Ed's daughter.

"Of course, I'm not pregnant. Not really pregnant, anyway."

"What do you mean, not really pregnant."

She was looking at me rather funny.

I then explained what was going on with the simulated pregnancy. I was supposed to be about three months along right now, so nothing was showing, although I could certainly feel the fullness inside my tummy. I was definitely growing.

"So how did Shawna find out."

"I told Ed. I needed to let him know that I was pregnant before we started making love so he wouldn't worry about it. Besides, it's part of my cover story that I was pregnant when my husband was killed."

"How far along are you supposed to be?"

"Three months."

"Three months?" she exclaimed. "You'll be in maternity clothes before long."

"Well, I can't wear my corset any more," I said, putting my hand on my tummy.

"What's going to happen when the due date comes around?"

"Well, I'll go away to visit my mother, or some story, and have the baby. Then, I'll either adopt a baby or I'll lose the baby."

"Oh, how sad," she frowned. "Don't lose the baby."

"I'll see in a few months. I don't know if I can handle a newborn, and the adoption may not work out."

"I'll help you."

"Thank you, Debbie," I smiled at her. "Did you know that I could actually nurse the baby?"

"No!" she looked at me like I was crazy. "Not really?"

"Yes, really. They'll give me a special hormone in addition to the ones I'm already taking and my milk glands start thinking I'm pregnant and will actually lactate."

"Oh, that's exciting. You'll have to have the baby, then."

"I'll keep thinking about it."

"You keep thinking about having a baby. I don't want to hear anything about losing a baby."

"Okay."

"Great. Can I tell everyone?"

"Sure. It shouldn't be a secret. I don't want people thinking Ed knocked me up or anything."

She reached out and put her hand on my stomach.

"This is so exciting," she said. "Let's go tell the girls, right now. They'll want to know right away."

"You are so impatient," I said, laughing along with her.

We walked back to the patio where several of our friends were chatting in a small circle.

"Ladies," Debbie announced. "Marcia has an important announcement to make."

The women all looked at me.

"Oh, Debbie," I was blushing. "She is so blunt about these things."

"All right, then," Debbie said. "Marcia won't tell you so I will. She is pregnant."

All the women immediately broke into smiles and reached out to hold my hands and give their congratulations.

Chapter 8

I was seven months pregnant and feeling every minute of it. I was quite large, but knew that I was going to get larger. My breasts had started to swell with the new hormones, although they weren't ready to lactate, yet. Debbie and Barbara had come over for tea and conversation when the phone rang.

"Hello," I said.

"Marcia," it was Ed's voice. "I was wondering if I could come over. I have something for you."

"Of course you can," I said, smiling. "Debbie and Barbara are over here, but I can ask them to leave."

"Oh, no," he said. "That's not necessary. They will probably like to see what I have for you."

"I can't wait."

"Bye."

I hung up and returned to the living room. My back hurt and I waddled a bit. I was wearing a maternity skirt and blouse that made me look even larger than I was.

"That was Ed," I said. "He's coming over to show me something."

"A gift?" Debbie asked.

"I don't know. He wouldn't tell me."

"I wonder what it could be," Barbara said.

"He's been leaving me a gift every time I turn around. I don't know what to say anymore."

"You say thank you and smile a lot," Debbie said with a big grin on her face.

Ed arrived about a half hour later and I showed him into the living room. He greeted my friends and then handed me a box. It was quite large, wrapped with a gold metallic paper. There was a large white satin bow on top with matching satin ribbon around the box.

"Oh, Ed," I exclaimed as I took it from him. "Whatever is this. You give me too many things."

"Nonsense," he said, smiling. "Sit down and open it. Your friends will want to see it."

I went to a rocking chair in the middle of the living room floor and sat down, holding the box on my lap. Carefully I took the bow off and laid it on the floor beside me. I took the ribbon off and then slowly unwrapped the paper, savoring every moment of the gift.

"I have always enjoyed watching women unwrap presents," Ed said to my friends. "It's always such a science."

"Oh, hush up, Ed," I said with a big grin. I could already see that the box was from one of my favorite shops downtown. He had spared no expense.

I took the wrapping paper off, laying it on the floor. Barbara and Debbie were exclaiming as they saw the name of the store, too.

"I couldn't afford to even go in the front door. Ed, how can you do this?" Debbie said, walking over to get a closer look.

"I want my beautiful girl to be even more beautiful."

"You just keep talking that way," I said.

I opened the box and was stunned. It was the most beautiful robe I had ever seen. It was of white satin with satin brocade along the front. The belt was of matching satin brocade. The collar was beautifully stitched satin with a lace overlay. It must have cost him over two hundred dollars.

"Oh, Ed," I was speechless.

"Oh, Marcia," Ed responded, smiling and enjoying my predicament.

"That's absolutely gorgeous," Debbie said, and Barbara agreed emphatically.

"You said you didn't have anything nice like that," Ed explained. "I wanted you to have a nice robe for the times you have to go to the hospital. I can't have my girl parading around in front of strangers looking like a slob."

I laid the robe back into the box and set it down. I got up and went to Ed and put my arms around his neck. He leaned over and we kissed. I have him a big hug and he hugged me back.

"Be careful, there," he said. "We don't want to get too close for the little one."

"The little one loves you, too, you crazy man."

Ed kissed me one more time.

"I have to go now," he said, moving toward the front door. "Just had enough time to drop by."

"When will I see you, again?" I asked.

"Probably tonight," he answered, smiling with that wonderful twinkle in his eye.

"I'll be here."

"Love you," and he was gone.

I turned back inside and looked once again at the beautiful robe. Ed loved to give me things. A week didn't go by that he didn't drop something off, but never had it been something so expensive as that robe. He was certainly getting more serious about me.

"I think he loves you a lot," Debbie said.

"I think Debbie is right," Barbara added. "You need to hang onto him."

"I'm planning on it," I said, looking at Debbie. Debbie's smile faded for just a second, but then returned. Her eyes were a bit sad.

"You two will be so happy together. I hope it all works out."

Debbie was putting on a brave face. She was obviously happy for me, but sad and a little jealous at the same time. We needed to talk, but there wasn't time right then. Barbara was so thrilled by all of it, and she was not aware of the past. Debbie and I would talk later.

The House on Sackett Street: A Love Story

Chapter 9

My belly hurt like the devil and I wasn't really sure I wanted to go on with this pregnancy thing. I had just returned from the doctor after my monthly "pre-natal" visit. As they had been doing for the past several months, they injected a bit more saline solution into the bladder inside my abdomen. I was quite swollen and did in fact appear to be about eight months pregnant. I was starting to walk with a bit of a waddle and my back had been hurting for some time. I had long since changed into maternity clothing. There was a nice side to all this, though. The attention I got from my friends was nice. Debbie and Barbara even had a baby shower scheduled. The part I still wasn't sure of was how all this was going to end in a few months when I was going to "deliver" my baby.

I was getting out of the car when I heard the voice behind me.

"Just be quiet and go into the house."

I didn't even see him, but the voice was that of a man, a bit raspy. I could sense that he was close behind, and even feel his breath on my neck. I moved toward the front door quickly, hoping that one of my neighbors would see what was going on and call the police.

"What do you want?" I was nearly in tears from fright.

"Just shut up and open the door."

His breath was stale with cigarette smoke and smelled of booze. He didn't sound drunk, but he had certainly been drinking. What did he want? I was afraid I knew.

I opened the door and we went in. He roughly shoved me inside, slammed the door and pushed me toward the back rooms.

"Where's your bedroom?"

"Straight ahead," I lied. I did not want to go into my own bedroom. I steered him toward the second bedroom.

He pushed me inside and roughly down onto the bed face down. Only then did I get a look at him. He was about 5 feet eight inches tall, slightly overweight and had not shaven for some days. Altogether a rough character.

"What do you want?" I asked again, this time nearly in tears.

"Take off your blouse."

His teeth were yellow and his hands were dirty.

"Take off your blouse, now, or I'll hurt you."

I started unbuttoning my blouse, a long maternity top. My hands were shaking and it was difficult to handle the buttons.

"Hurry up, bitch. I wanna see those udders of yours."

I got the buttons undone and opened the front of my top. I left it on.

"Take it off."

I slipped it off my shoulders, turning slightly sideways to hide my front from his leering eyes.

"Now take off the bra."

I reached behind me and, as quickly as my shaking hands would allow, unclasped my bra, letting it slide down my arms. My breasts, quite large from the hormones, fell down.

The man moved forward and reached out his hand, touching my right breast roughly. He ran his fingers over my nipple and then roughly squeezed the breast.

"Ouch," I yelled sharply. "That hurts."

"Yeah," I bet it does, bitch. Got yourself knocked up and now your boobs hurt, huh?"

I tried to turn away from him to keep him from hurting my breasts any more. He pushed me back on the bed.

"Now take your skirt off."

I was wearing a maternity skirt and it slipped off easily, leaving me in a half slip.

"Take the rest off. I wanna see the rest."

As slowly as I could I pushed the half slip down. I slipped my shoes off and then just sat there. I still had my panties on.

"Off with the panties. I wanna see it all, bitch."

"Don't call me that name," I said back to him, by now crying quite hard.

"Just get those off and let me see your knocked up pussy."

I slipped the panties off and sat on the bed naked in front of this horrible creature. I couldn't bring myself to even think of being raped by him.

He walked forward and put his hand on my belly. Then he ran it down toward my legs and started to touch my pubic hair. Roughly, he pushed my legs apart and placed his hand between my legs. He pushed a finger inside me. It hurt, there being no lubrication. I cried at the hurting.

"Shut up," he yelled, and then he hit me across the face with the back of his hand. I fell back onto the bed. He pushed his finger further up inside me, hurting even more.

Then, he stood up, and took his trousers down. He wasn't wearing any under shorts and his penis was erect, already dripping. I cried as I imagined what he was about to do. I tried to crawl away from him, but he grabbed my leg and pulled me back. I screamed and he hit me across the face, and I screamed again. All I could imagine was what he was about to do to me.

He grabbed at me and roughly pulled my legs apart and started to crawl on top of me. He lay heavily on my stomach and I hurt badly. The pain shot up through me like fire as he put nearly his full weight on my extended belly.

Then I heard a loud crash. He fell on me with his full weight for a second, and then the weight lifted.

"Are you okay, Marcia?"

I heard the voice, but it didn't register right away.

"Are you okay, Marcia?" it said again, "Marcia?"

"I..I'm okay...I guess."

I then knew what I was hearing. It was Barbara's husband.

"Get that creep out of here so Marcia doesn't have to see him."

"Here, put this on."

He handed me my robe which had been hanging on the back of the door. I quickly pulled it on, tying the belt around my waist. I was still sobbing and wasn't really hearing or seeing anything straight.

"We'll take care of that guy. The police will be here in a minute."

There were several other people in the room. There was Phil, Barbara's husband, and there was Tom, from across the street, and then I saw Barbara.

"Oh, Barbara," I started crying again.

"Marcia," she came to me and held me tight.

Chapter 10

It was time to leave to "have my baby." I had the plane ticket back to the town where my "sister" lived. I had packed two suitcases and had my overnight bag ready to go. All the arrangements were made with the service and the hospital. I would be picked up at the airport by one of the officers and taken to the hospital. I would be admitted as a maternity patient with complications, probably requiring a caesarian delivery. Then, after the operation, they would bring in the baby I was to adopt.

Debbie called me early that morning.

"I'm going with you, Marcia."

"I don't think you can do that."

"Of course I can. I am going with you. What do you know about having babies?"

"I know as much as you did when you had your first one."

"True," she chuckled. "But, I'm still coming with you."

"Let me check on it, first."

"Nonsense. I already have the ticket."

We both arrived at the airport together. Two 40ish women, one of whom as obviously pregnant and not altogether comfortable. My belly was swollen and my back hurt most of the time. Debbie assured me it was normal, but that didn't help my attitude any. Actually I was excited about getting the baby. I had been taking the extra hormones for the past month and I knew my breasts were already lactating. I

was able to manually get some milk to come out of my nipple when I worked at it.

"Now, here we are," Debbie said as we settled into our seats

"My belly hurts," was all I could say.

"Not for long."

"Not for long, you say. It will hurt like hell after the c section."

"That will be different."

"You never had a c section."

"True, but you'll survive."

We settled into our seats. The flight attendants were very nice to me, curious about me and my pregnancy. Soon we arrived at our destination.

"They're going to have a cow when you come off the plane with me."

"They won't have a chance to do anything about it."

"I hope you're right, Debbie."

"I am."

"I'm glad you're with me, Debbie."

She smiled.

"I'm happy to be here with you. I wouldn't have it any other way."

The plane arrived at the gate and soon we were walking down the ramp. We were met by a man who quickly identified me.

"Mrs. Marcia Stephens?"

"Yes," I answered. "I'm Mrs. Stephens."

"Hello," he smiled, putting out his hand. "I'm Tom Larson. I'm to take you to the hospital."

"Thank you. This is my friend Debbie Watson. She will be helping me."

"Oh, yes. We've been expecting you, Mrs. Watson."

I looked over at Debbie. She smiled and shrugged her shoulders.

"You had this planned all along, didn't you."

"Sure did, Mrs. Stephens."

Debbie still got a kick out of hearing me called Mrs. Stephens.

We followed our guide to a car. He had already arranged to have our luggage picked up, and soon we were on our way out of the airport. It took about half an hour to arrive at the hospital. It wasn't a public institution, but it was certainly modern. I remembered it distinctly from my long stay here last year.

"Is this where you had your operations?" Debbie asked.

"Yes. I was in here for what seemed like forever."

"Well, this won't take forever."

"I hope not. I just want to get this over with and be a mom."

"I still can't get over you being a mother."

"Neither can I. But it does sound exciting."

"Exciting? I haven't heard it called that."

We laughed and soon were getting out of the car at the front entrance of the hospital.

"Hello, Mrs. Stephens."

The voice was familiar. I looked up and it was a nurse I remembered from before.

"Oh, hi," I answered. "I forget your name, but I do remember you."

"I'm Anne Locklear. I'll be your nurse and natal care instructor."

"Well, I'm sure I'll need all the instruction I can get."

"You are looking very good. Your new life is agreeing with you."

"As soon as I have this baby, I'll be even better."

They rolled a wheelchair out for me and I sat down. Debbie followed as Anne pushed me into the hospital. They took me up to the maternity ward, checked me in, and assigned me a room.

"So when is the operation scheduled?" I asked Anne.

"Tomorrow morning. You can go anywhere you want in the hospital tonight. Don't eat anything after six o'clock. We'll get you up at five and you'll be in the operating room by six. It won't take long, and by noon you'll be fully awake and have a new little baby. Is it a girl or a boy?"

"A girl."

"And you already have a pink room for it at home, right?"

"As a matter of fact I do."

She smiled, showed me where to put a few things, then left Debbie and I alone.

"Scared?" Debbie asked.

"A little," I answered. I went to a chair and sat down.

"My feet are killing me," I said as I slipped my shoes off.

"I know what you mean. I never should have worn these heels."

"What's it like nursing a baby?"

"It's wonderful. It feels wonderful and makes you feel very feminine and loving."

"I can't wait. Besides, my breasts hurt. They're full of milk. I think they gave me a double dose of those hormones."

"Get used to that feeling for a while."

"So, what should we do? Are you hungry?"

"It's three o'clock, so if we are going to eat, we'd better do it now."

"I saw a cafeteria downstairs."

"Alright, I'll put my shoes back on and we'll go get something to eat."

We walked down the hall to the elevator, took it down two floors, and found the cafeteria. We had a nice lunch, although I didn't eat too much, knowing that they would be putting me under some anesthesia the next morning.

"Debbie," I said as we were walking back to the room. "I want to tell you that you are the most wonderful woman in the world."

"Well, thank you, Mrs. Stephens. Why on earth do you think that?"

"How many women would marry a man, live with him for twenty years, then watch him turn into a woman, make love with her, and help her have a baby?"

"Not too many, I suppose."

"I suppose not."

"But, I love you, Marcia."

"I love you too, Debbie. I always have."

"I love you as Marcia, though. Mark is finally dead, I think."

"I suppose he is. You know, I want to marry Ed. I want my baby to have a father."

"I know you do. I think Ed wants to marry you, too. Have you told him about yourself?"

"No. Not yet. I haven't figured out how."

"Don't worry. The right time will come. I'll be your matron of honor."

I smiled, we hugged, and we kissed.

Chapter 11

I went into the operating room the next morning and they took out the balloon. They used an incision just like a caesarian section, and then sewed me back up. I woke up in my room with Debbie looking over me.

"Debbie," I was still a bit bleary eyed.

"I'm here Marcia. You did just fine and you have your girlish figure back."

I smiled at that and reached out to take her hand.

She held my hand and I just closed my eyes to rest. I could hardly move and when I did my tummy hurt like the devil. Then it came to me.

"I'm a mother!"

"That's right, Marcia. A proud mother."

"When do I see my baby?"

"Later when you are more awake."

"Oh, I want to see my baby now."

"They'll bring her down in an hour for feeding."

"Feeding?"

"That's right. You'll be breast feeding."

I then realized that part of the discomfort I was feeling was my breasts. They were heavy and full of milk. The last several days the doctors had increased the hormone dosage and my breasts were making milk full time. They hurt and I needed to have them emptied.

"Oh, Debbie, I can't wait an hour. My breasts hurt too much."

"You can wait," Debbie said as she smiled, still holding my hand.

I reached up and rubbed my breast. It was a little sore, but as I lay there, I found that the pressure wasn't as bad as I thought.

"What's it like to nurse a baby?" I asked.

"It's wonderful," Debbie sat back in her chair. "It's the best feeling in the world."

"I remember you always enjoyed it."

"I did. And you will, too."

Exactly at the appointed hour, the nurse brought my little baby daughter in to me. All the adoption arrangements had been made well ahead of time and the baby brought to the hospital the same day I arrived. She was only four days old, having been born to a young girl in another hospital across town. She was so cute in the blanket.

The nurse handed her to me and I nestled her into my arms. She immediately started hunting for my breast.

"She knows what to do," I exclaimed.

"She does indeed. Now open your gown so she can get some dinner."

I reached up and opened the placket in my gown, exposing my breast. As soon as I placed my baby to my breast, she latched onto my nipple and began sucking away.

Suddenly I felt a funny feeling in my breast. It was as though all the milk suddenly had a mind of its own and began falling from my breast.

"Oh," I said, surprised. "I think I just let down."

"It couldn't happen at a better time."

"But, I think my other breast is leaking, now."

Sure enough, while the baby was suckling at my right breast, my left breast was leaking milk, soaking my gown.

"Well, Marcia," Debbie was grinning. "It happens to the best of us."

I was so happy. My newborn baby was suckling at my breast, drinking real mothers milk. I settled back against the pillow and just let my daughter drink from my breast. There was no happier mother in the world at that instant.

Chapter 12

Ed came over to my house on Friday evening as he often did. I was very
anxious. The time had come to deal with my past and to tell Ed about my
background. Our relationship had grown very serious. He dearly loved Emily
and would dote over her as if her were the biological father. I loved seeing it, but
feared the moment when I would have to tell him. There was no doubt in my
mind that I had to tell him.

I just could not go on loving him and be able to keep that large a secret.

Our opening conversation was much as it usually was, discussion of the week's
events and what had happened to each of us. He always checked up on Emily,
usually feeding her if it was time. He loved to rock her to sleep. Finally, Ed

sensed that something was on my mind.

"You are wanting to talk about something very serious, aren't you?" he said, in a
matter of fact tone.

I was facing the sink at that moment, washing some glasses. I said nothing for a
few seconds. Then, with a deep breath, I turned around.

"Ed," I always started a sentence with his name if I was serious. "We need to
talk. Let's go into the living room."

He looked at me with a troubled expression, not knowing how to take it. I put
the dishtowel I had been using on the counter and led him into the other room. I
sat on my favorite rocking chair. Ed sat in the large overstuffed chair which he
had "claimed" as his own.

"This sounds very serious," he said, looking directly at me. It was going to be
hard for me.

"It is very serious," I said, my voice starting to choke. "It may even mean the
end of our relationship."

"What do you mean?" he was obviously shocked. "Surely nothing is that
serious."

"This is something you would never have thought about," I went on, my voice still giving me trouble. "But, I must tell you before we go any further with our relationship. It's unfair for you not to know."

Ed was silent, just looking at me, still very troubled.

"I have not told you everything about my past. Some things I told you about my past are not even true."

"Like what?" he asked.

"Like my entire childhood," I responded. "Like most of my adult life."

"What on earth are you talking about, Marcia?"

"I'm talking about the biggest lie in the world. I'm talking about what you think about me," I was nearly hysterical and was starting to cry.

"Come, now, Marcia," he stood up and started to walk over to me. "Nothing is this bad."

"Please, Ed," I said, wiping away tears, "sit down. I need to tell you something about me that will shock you."

"Alright," he answered and returned to the chair.

"A year ago I was involved in a special government operation in Colombia against one of the drug cartels."

Ed was looking very seriously at me. I continued.

"The result was very good, and several of the drug lords were arrested. You probably heard about it on the news."

He nodded imperceptibly.

"I was in very great danger of being hunted down by the men we did not get, so the government put me in a very special protection program. We did some unprecedented things to ensure that they could not find me like they had found other agents and officers involved in such operations before."

"So you are using an assumed name?" he asked.

"Yes," I nodded.

"That's not so bad."

"That's only part of it, Ed," I started crying, again. "When I did those things last year, I wasn't what you see here. I was a man."

Ed just stared at me. He did not say a word. I was completely in tears. I could not even look at him.

"I will understand if you just leave and never see me again," I said through the sobs.

He still did not answer.

I looked up at him.

He looked at me and finally spoke.

"You mean to say that you were once a man, and now you have had the surgery to become a woman?"

"Yes," I answered. "That's true."

"What about Emily? You were pregnant."

"All part of the show. I adopted her."

"But, you were really pregnant. I mean, your belly and everything." Ed was starting to lose coherency.

"I can tell you all the details if you want to hear them, but what I am saying is true."

"This is pretty difficult to take, you know."

"I know," I nodded, still wiping my eyes. "I know."

"I couldn't tell the difference, Marcia."

His voice was different. It was not as hard as a few seconds before. I just looked at him, silently.

"You have been a wonderful woman to me. And a wonderful mother to Emily. You have breastfed her, and taken care of her. You have loved me."

I could say nothing. I did not know where he was going.

"Marcia," he said, standing up. He started to walk toward me. "This is hard for me to understand, but you have to realize something."

"Understand something?"

"You must understand that I have loved you from when I first talked to you at church. I have loved you more every day we have been together and I will continue to love you."

"I don't understand. I have been lying to you."

"And I understand why. How could you have told me all this when we first me. We didn't know each other. Now, we know each other intimately. This is just a small hurdle. Just one more thing we have learned about each other. There will be others, and we will get over them, too."

"Ed," I couldn't say anything else.

"Marcia," Ed took hold of my shoulders. "I love you."

"Oh, Ed," I stopped trying to hold back the tears. "I love you so much. I don't want to lose you."

"And I don't want to lose you either, Marcia."

He held me close, and I just lay my head on his shoulder, crying my eyes out. I did not know whether I was happy or sad. I did know that I was in love and that I had found a very special man.

"Marcia," he went on. "Let's get you cleaned up and we'll talk about all this some more. I'm sure you have lots to tell me and I want to hear it all."

We did talk. We talked all night and I told him everything. He was curious about all of it and I held back on nothing.

I looked at the clock and it was midnight. We had been talking for several hours. I was sitting next to him on the couch, exhausted mentally from all that I had explained. I leaned my head on his shoulder and just luxuriated in his presence, feeling his warmth against my cheek.

He touched my face with his hand, then touched my breast. I looked up at him.

"Do you still want me?" I asked. "Do you still want me after all you know about me?"

"Of course I do, Marcia."

"Really?"

"Really," he said. "I only know you as a woman. I cannot even imagine you as a man. It is meaningless to me."

I smiled and laid my head back on his shoulder.

"I do need one thing, though.'

"What?" I looked up at him, curious.

"I need to see you. I need to see all of you. Naked. Right now."

I smiled and stood up. I would undress for him. He needed to see me and I wanted to make him happy. I started to unbutton my blouse. I could see his eyes hungrily look at me. I slowly undid the front of my blouse, just allowing a hint of my bra to show. Then I unzipped my skirt, letting it slowly drop down my hips, just letting him catch a peek of my slip as the skirt slowly dropped to the floor.

I stood before him with my blouse open in front, my half slip covering my nether regions, teasing him with what lay beneath. I reached up behind my back and unhooked my bra, letting it hang loosely in front. I shook my shoulders. My breasts shook, just allowing a peek of my nipples as they sprang free of the lacy cover of my pretty bra.

I pushed the slip down my hips, carefully controlling it so he could see the lace of my panties begin to show slowly. I dropped the slip to the floor then shrugged my shoulders to let the blouse and bra fall away, exposing my breasts to his view.

I shook my shoulders again, letting my breasts wiggle in front of his eyes. I could see a lump growing in his pants, a small wet spot on the front of his trousers. I was getting excited, too.

I walked up to him and reached down to his belt. I unbuckled it and then unzipped his pants. With a quick pull, I removed his pants, leaving his only in his shirt and underpants, the latter with a huge tent pole holding them up. My tongue licked my lips seeing the growing wet spot on the white cotton under shorts.

I stepped back and then pushed my panties down, exposing myself to Ed. He looked at me. He looked at the pubic hair and the pink labia peeking out. He reached down and pushed his under shorts off and I saw his wonderful erection, so huge and ready for me.

I kneeled down in front of him and took that great penis into my mouth. It was so soft and I ran my tongue along its length, savoring its flavor, now getting more and more familiar. Ed moaned and ran his fingers through my hair, holding my head so I couldn't get away from the wonderful feelings I was causing him. Not that I wanted to get away, as I really enjoyed going down on him. His hips were beginning to buck as the excitement built inside him. I took the penis all the way inside my mouth, all the way to the back of my throat. I gagged a little, but kept working it in and out of my mouth, holding his testicles in one hand, tickling between his legs with the other.

A memory flashed in my mind. I remembered my wife doing the same thing to me, and how much I loved it. Never in my life did I imagine loving this so much. All I wanted to do was make this wonderful man come and then take him inside my waiting vagina.

`Ed began making more noises. He was close to the end and I didn't want it to quit so soon. I took my mouth off his penis and leaned up to kiss him. I sat on his lap and rubbed his penis with my legs, rocking my bottom along his thighs and then his erection. I could feel it between my legs and along my thighs. I could feel him pushing with his hips as though to force his penis inside me. I felt the warm, soft tip

of his penis brush my bottom and I knew I needed him inside me right then.

`I pulled him off the couch and I lay back on the floor, my legs spread wide. He looked down at me and smiled. He reached down with his hand and slipped a finger inside me.

I closed my eyes and moaned loudly.

"Ed, if you don't screw me right now I'll scream."

"So scream," Ed said. "I want to hear you scream."

So I screamed. I let out a shriek that must have been heard all the way down the street. And Ed entered me as I screamed, which made me scream even louder, feeling his warm, smooth, hard erection slide inside my very willing vagina.

Chapter 13

Debbie arrived just after ten and we were in the car heading into town just a few minutes later. Barbara was watching my baby and told Debbie and I to stay gone all day. Our destination was Pierre's, a bridal salon we had picked out some days before. We were on our way to try on a wedding gown and have it fit.

We parked behind the shop and walked around to the front. It wasn't a large place, but was completely packed full of gowns of all sorts. There were wedding gowns of all types, bridesmaids gowns, formal ball gowns, cocktail dresses. We knew exactly the one, however, and went straight to the shop keeper.

"Good afternoon," I said. "I'm Marcia Stephens. I have an appointment to fit a wedding gown."

The woman looked into a small book, closed it, looked up at me, smiled and said, "If you'll just come this way."

We followed her into the back where she pointed us to a fitting room. In the room was hanging the dress. I was still overwhelmed by its beauty. I was also overwhelmed by its expense, but that was going to be taken care of by the service.

"Oh, Marcia, it's so beautiful."

I could only nod as I went over to look at it. The bodice was of beaded raw silk with lace overlay. The collar was of high lace, and buttoned down the back. The skirts were of raw silk, all white, with a huge bow on the back. The sleeves were of the same white silk with lace overlays. I couldn't believe that I was actually going to wear this dress to a wedding...my own wedding.

"Well, lets get this lovely thing on you," Debbie prompted.

I put my purse down, and unbuttoned my blouse. I hung it on the rack provided and quickly shed my skirt as well. I was dressed in the underwear for the gown. I had on a white lace corset that held my breasts up and my waist in. The panties were white lace over white panty hose. I took a pair of white satin shoes from my carry bag and slipped them on.

I slipped on the full petticoats that would fill out the skirts. They were of crinoline and lace. Debbie already had the dress off the hanger for me to put on.

I held my arms out and slipped them under the skirts of the dress. It was heavy. The raw silk was very heavy, not as light as some of the satin dresses I had tried on. I thought that the raw silk was more elegant, especially for an older woman like myself.

The dress was on in an instant, and Debbie was buttoning up the back. The attendant attached the bow and I stood in front of the mirror. I was breathless at how pretty the dress was. It was all I could do to keep tears back.

The attendant quickly began working around me, checking the waist and the length. After some pinning and marking, she announced that she was done and I could take it off.

Debbie and I walked out of the store a little later chatting up a storm about wedding plans.

"So who else will you have a bridesmaids?"

"Barbara and Shawna. That's all."

"That's okay, I guess. Is Ed only having three men?"

"Yes. Tom, his brother is his best man, and two of his friends."

"Are they cute?"

"Yes, Debbie," I laughed at her. "They're cute."

The next stop was a lingerie store. I wanted a new nightgown for my wedding night and I had spotted the right one at a little store on Main Street. I took it out of the box and held it up for Debbie to see.

"Oh, Marcia," she smiled, "that won't stay on for thirty seconds."

"That's the idea, I guess. That's what you always told me."

The gown was really sexy. It was white, of course, and of sheer lace and nylon. The gown was completely sheer and deeply cut in front with a high waist. The robe was a little more opaque, with satin sleeves and waist band. My breasts would be held out for Ed to see and would be able to see my pubic patch easily through the thin material. I would be the most scrumptious thing on his plate that night.

I paid for it and we headed back to the house. It didn't take long and we pulled up and headed in.

"Marcia," Debbie said. She was serious.

"Yes, Debbie?" I sat down, motioning her to do the same.

"I am so happy for you. I think you and Ed are going to have a great time together."

"Thank you. I think we will be great together, too."

"I want you to know that I am not jealous and I really want things to go well for you."

"I know you do."

"I want you to know that I still love you, though."

"And I love you, too, Debbie. I love you a lot."

She leaned over and kissed me on the cheek. I kissed her back and we hugged briefly.

"I still want to be able to make love with you," Debbie said. "Even after you are married."

I was quiet for a second.

"I mean that, Marcia. I know that sounds terrible, but I need to know that you will still want to make love to me."

"How can I do that, Debbie? I'll be married."

"We can do it. Ed will never know."

"Debbie," I stood up. "Ed does know all about me. He even knows that you were my wife."

It was her turn to be silent.

"He does?"

"Yes, he knows. I had to tell him everything so I would be sure about our love. I couldn't hold any secrets from him."

"Does he know that we've made love. I mean, made love since your operation?"

"Yes. He knows."

"And he doesn't mind?"

"He did, at first. He had a hard time with that one."

"I think he's a really great guy."

I agreed. This was going to be hard. I really wanted to remain close to Debbie, but I also wanted to be faithful to my new husband. I didn't know how to handle it.

"You do understand that I have to be faithful to Ed, don't you."

"Of course I understand," Debbie was getting a little testy. "You were supposed to be faithful to me, remember."

She had me there. While the official death had technically ended our marriage, there I was alive and well with no divorce papers or anything else ending our marriage.

"So, if we can still make love, that would keep you happy?"

"Yes. I need to stay close to you. I want to be able to see you and make love to you whenever we can. I understand you want to be with Ed. I really do understand. You should be faithful to him. Don't do anything with any other man. Just keep me in mind. This isn't the most routine situation, you know."

I stood quietly and looked at her. She was right. This was not just a standard situation of a woman getting married to a man she loved. I was really still married to this woman in my living room, and I wanted to marry a man I loved.

"Debbie," I walked over to her and held out my hands.

"I love you. I will always love you. I want to be able to make love to you anytime we need it. I will always keep you close to my heart."

"Marcia," she was crying. "I love you, too. I promise I won't be jealous of Ed. Trust me."

"We will have to be sure Ed doesn't get suspicious."

"Ed will be just fine."

"Kiss me, Debbie."

We embraced and kissed long and deep. Her hands went to my breasts and mine up under her skirt. Quickly I found her moist panties and slipped my finger up inside her warm love nest. She melted into my arms and kissed me even harder. Her hands groped up under my skirt. She rubbed softly between my legs. She rubbed against the lace of my panties and tried to run her fingers under them. My pantyhose stopped her from what she was groping for. She kissed me harder.

"Marcia," Debbie said, almost breathless. "I need you. I need you right now."

"I need you, too, Debbie," I was getting hot. I moved her hands to my panties and let her pull them down. Then, I hooked my fingers around the waist of my pantyhose and started to roll them down. I kicked my heels off and she helped me take my pantyhose off. Her lips went straight for my love nest and she kissed my clitoris. It was almost more than I could take.

"I need to get you moist," Debbie said.

"I am already."

"You must have known."

"I knew. I knew."

She slipped her finger up inside me and I nearly came on the spot. I could feel her up inside me and I wanted to be inside her. I wished I had a penis again so I could be inside her like I used to be able. Then I felt something different.

"What are you doing?" I said.

"I'm coming inside you. The only way I can."

"Coming inside me?"

"Coming inside you. It's my way of giving you back some of what you were able to give me."

She was pushing a dildo up inside me. It was large and filled me completely. She moved it around and in and out and I fell back breathless with Debbie moving the artificial penis inside me.

"Debbie," I was nearly speechless. "Debbie, this is wonderful. I have to do it to you."

"You just lay there and take it, Marcia. I want you to feel me inside you."

I lay there with my eyes closed. I felt the false penis moving inside me. She knew exactly where to move it. She touched my clitoris with her fingers and then licked it with her tongue. I was nearing the edge. I grabbed her head and pulled it down to me and kissed her. I rubbed her breasts and ran my hands down between her legs. She was soaking wet.

Her panties were wet and I could easily push the nylon of her panties up inside her. She moaned. She moved the dildo one more time and then touched my clitoris at just the right moment and I came with a crash. I could only hear a loud rush in my head as the feeling came over me in a rush. I grabbed her and pulled her to me. She

kept moving the dildo around inside me, but I just wanted her close.

"Oh, Debbie," I was breathless. "That was wonderful. I have to do you, now."

"No," she smiled and slowly removed the dildo from my soaking wet vagina. "Not now. I just want to look at you. Let me see your new nightgown."

"Right now?" I was still out of breath. All I could think of was getting hold of Debbie and making more love to her.

"I want to see how pretty you are in your new nightgown. I want to see how Ed will see you on your wedding night."

"Okay," I said, and got up. I went to the dresser and took it from the package. I took the corset off and then slipped the gown over my head. It was low enough for the cleavage of my breasts to show very nicely. It was sheer enough that my nipples and my pubic hair showed through, too. Debbie was licking her lips.

"Now put on the robe."

I pulled it on. It closed with a small tie at the waist and a waistband of satin. My cleavage still showed nicely and just a hint of my nipples and pubic hair showed. It felt wonderful as it flowed around my naked body, still tingling with the rush of my climax. Debbie was still hungry for me.

She got up from the bed and walked over to me. She unbuttoned her blouse and let it drop to the floor. She unhooked her skirt and let it join the blouse. She was in front of me in just her bra and panties. They were a pretty set of pale pink nylon, satin and lace. Her breasts jutted up for me to see and her panties were soaked through. I could see liquid running down the inside of her thigh. She was hotter than I was, if possible.

"Oh, Marcia, I never thought I could get so hot for another woman."

"I never thought you could either," I answered. I looked down at myself. My breasts were heaving with my own excitement. I could feel my own juices, artificial as they were, running down my own thighs. I wanted to taste Debbie. She wanted to taste me. I wanted to be beautiful for her.

"Marcia," Debbie was standing directly in front of me. She leaned over and pulled her panties off. I reached forward and unhooked her bra. It fell from her breasts.

"Marcia," she repeated. "I don't want to lose you. I want you forever. I'll even share you with Ed. Just don't forget me."

"I'll never forget you."

"I'll always remember you as a man. Now I'll remember you as a woman."

"I'll always remember you as my wife. Even when I'm married to Ed, I'll remember what it was like. I will always love you, Debbie."

"Keep saying that, Marcia. Keep saying that."

She was getting closer. She moved her hands to my breasts. I could feel her fingers barely touching me through the material of the nightgown.

"You are so beautiful in this gown."

"You are so beautiful just standing there naked."

She held my left breast with her right hand.

"Your breasts are so large. So much larger than mine. Ed must love them."

"He does. He loves them just like I have always loved yours."

"Mine are so small."

"Yours are beautiful. I have always loved yours."

I held her breasts with my hands. I brushed the nipples with my palms. She shivered and closed her eyes, still holding my left breast. Her other hand went down between my legs. She pushed the material of my robe aside and ran her hand up between my legs. I could feel the soft material of the nightgown against my thighs as she cupped my love triangle with her palm. She moved her fingers ever so slightly and I began to shiver with excitement. She leaned forward, eyes still closed, and we kissed. My breasts pressed against hers, the nightgown sliding luxuriously between our bodies. My nipples were tender and wanted to be touched. My vagina ached to have her fingers and lips touch it. My own tongue wanted to taste her womanhood. We did all that, and much more.

Chapter 14

"Okay, Debbie," I said. "You have to lace my corset, now. Really tight so I can fit into this dress."

"Really tight so your boobs will make Ed hungry with lust, you mean," she laughed as she came over to help me.

"You're right, like always."

Debbie and I were in the bridal dressing room at the church. I was in my garters, hose, panties and heels, with my corset held out in front of me. It was a pretty corset of white satin with lace overlay. The bra cups were low cut to push my breasts up into a very alluring cleavage that would show nicely with the wedding gown.

Debbie came up behind me and as I held the corset in place, she laced it tightly.

"Is that tight enough?"

"More," I said. "I can still breath. I want the tiniest waist I can have today."

She finished lacing it up and I looked at myself in the mirror. I was in all white underwear, ravishing in satin and lace. My hair was pulled back and a white satin and raw silk bow was at the back of my neck. My ears were adorned with dangling white pearl earrings. My makeup was perfect. My eyes looked wide and alert. I looked ten years younger.

"Well, should we call Barbara and Shawna in to help put on the dress?" I asked. "They wanted to be here."

"I have something for you first."

I turned and looked at her. She was beautiful. She was wearing the pink gown we had selected for her. It was of the same raw silk as my dress. It was full in the sleeves and cut nearly as low as mine. The skirts were not as full as mine, but the petticoats gave it a nice sweep when she moved. She wore the same pearl earrings that I had on.

"What's that, Debbie?"

"I want to give you something special for your special day."

She held out her hand. In it was something I hadn't seen in years. Over twenty years, in fact. It was a pair of white lace panties. The very same panties she wore under her wedding dress when we were married. I remembered taking them off of her on our honeymoon.

"I want you to wear these. It will make you remember that we are still one together."

"Oh, Debbie. I didn't know you still had these."

"I always kept them packed in with my dress."

"You opened it up?"

She nodded. She held the panties out to me. I took them. They were very pretty. They were of white lace with a sheer nylon crotch and seat. Tiny pink bows were at each hip and a tiny rose was embroidered in the front.

"Are you sure?" I asked, holding the dainty thing in my hand.

"I am sure," she nodded. "Here, let me help you off with these."

She leaned over and slid my own panties down. She put them into her purse.

"I'll keep these and wear them to remind me of you."

"Help me slip these on. I can hardly lean over with this corset."

"First you need something else."

"Something else. Don't tell me you're going to give me all your underwear."

Oh, don't be silly," she said, opening her purse. She reached in and took out a tube of vaginal jelly.

"Ed is going to want to screw your brains out as soon as you get to your hotel and you won't have time for this. Let me get you ready ahead of time."

Before I could say anything, she had put a sizable amount of the jelly on her fingers and was rubbing it up inside me. Old feelings came back and I shivered with excitement. My face flushed as I felt her fingers touch my private parts, slipping fingers up inside my warm vagina, getting hotter as she rubbed the jelly into my most private parts.

"Debbie," I couldn't finish, I was so excited.

"Hush," Debbie said, putting her finger to my lips. She took her hand away from my crotch.

"Now," she continued, "let me help you put on your panties. Ed will want a hot, wet woman after you are married."

She leaned over and helped me slip the panties up my legs. They were a little tight, but they felt so good against my hot love nest. I could feel the jelly melting inside me. My panties were already getting wet. I felt so good. I felt so excited. I felt so female.

"That's your 'something old.' What about the other things?" Debbie asked.

"Well, 'something new' is the dress. 'Something borrowed' is the handkerchief you loaned me. And 'something blue' is the stone on my necklace."

"That should do it," Debbie stepped back and looked at me. "You are beautiful, Marcia. As beautiful as that picture on the wall in your house."

"Well, not that beautiful," I protested.

"Yes, you are," Debbie was almost serious. "This time you are really in love. That makes you even more beautiful."

I smiled. She smiled. We hugged and kissed each other on the cheek. Debbie was such a wonderful woman. Once my wife, now my dearest friend, practically a sister.

"Now, I'll get Barbara and Shawna," Debbie said and went to the door to call them in.

It didn't take long for the four of us to get me into my wedding gown. They touched up my makeup and checked my hair. They straightened my skirts and made sure everything was perfect. Then, it was time.

The wedding was beautiful, of course. Nearly all of my friends were there. Ed's family was there. Even my family was there. The service had seen to it that they had officers there acting as my son and daughter. My "daughter," a lovely young woman, held my baby. My "son," a handsome young man, sat next to her, and there were lots of people there from the church.

I walked down the aisle by myself. Ed was at the other end, so handsome in his white tuxedo. I didn't even hear the organ playing. I had other music in my ears. Music for Ed and music for a wonderful new life together with him and my new baby.

Chapter 15

We left the church in the limousine. I was still in my wedding gown and Ed in his white tuxedo. He was absolutely handsome, and I was the happiest woman in the world. Ed leaned over and kissed me as soon as the door shut and I held his head tightly. I didn't want him to quit. He tasted so good.

His hand moved along my waist and up my side. In a move so familiar to me by then, he slipped his hand up to my front and let his fingers dip down inside the bodice of my dress and into my brassiere. He brushed my nipples and my crotch came on fire. I pulled his mouth tighter to mine and my right hand moved to his lap. I could feel his wonderful erection growing beneath my hand. I was so much in love.

We were taken to the Royale Hotel and Ed swept me up to a wonderful honeymoon suite that must have cost him a fortune. He led me into the room and showed me around. He stopped and looked at me.

"I love you, Marcia. I love you so much."

"Then make love to me right now."

"Right now?"

"Right now. Right here."

He moved toward me, starting to undo his tie. I reached up under my dress and pulled my panties down. I was wearing stockings and a garter belt, so I was naked underneath. I held the panties up for him.

"Take me right here. Right now."

He unzipped his pants and with a quick movement out sprang his penis. That wonderful organ I had come to love so much. I couldn't wait to feel it inside me.

"Sit down on that chair," I said as I pointed to an armless chair by the window.

He went over and sat down, his erection pointing nearly straight up in the air. I walked over, pulled up my dress, and moved over the top of him. I held his penis in my right hand and slowly moved it around the lips of my vagina, putting moisture in all the right places. Then, with one move, I sat on him, letting him move all the way up inside my waiting love nest. My skirts spread out over us both, nearly covering everything.

Ed let out a moan as I engulfed his penis. He moved his hips to meet me as I took him all the way in. I moved up and down, savoring every feeling of his penis as it rubbed my insides. It was all Ed could do to sit still. He was ready and within ten seconds came with a loud groan. I could feel his semen explode inside me. I could feel it running out of my vagina. I could feel him pulsing inside me. It was the most fulfilling feeling I could imagine. I continued to ride up and down along that hard erection, letting it come nearly all the way out, touching the lips of my labia, then pushing down, forcing it all the way up inside my body. I never felt more like I was part of Ed than with his penis inside me.

I just sat there on his lap, his still hard penis impaling me, giving us both wonderful feelings. We kissed. We fondled each other. We hugged. He kissed the tops of my breasts. I licked his ears and kissed his neck. He ran his hands along my sides, across my chest and brushed my nipples. I shivered and started moving up and down on his hard penis again. I rocked my hips forward and backward to place my clitoris in just the right place. I was getting hotter and hotter. I was moving faster and faster. I was breathing harder and harder. I rocked, back and forth. I moved up and down. I could feel his penis moving inside me. I could feel the wetness growing as his juices spread inside and leaked outside. I could hear the sucking noise as we moved apart and could feel the head of his penis rub the inside of my vagina.

I leaned down and kissed him hard as I felt the climax coming and then suddenly I came with the loudest crash of my life. I screamed, then kissed him again, harder than ever before. Then, Ed came again, bucking his hips up into me with more strength than I could remember. I felt another gush of warm liquid leap inside me. I felt the warmness spread throughout my belly. I collapsed onto him, holding him tightly, his wonderful, hard, erect penis holding me onto his strong, masculine lap. I was truly in love with a truly wonderful man.

He leaned over and kissed my neck. Then, carefully, he picked me up. His penis pulled slowly out of me, and he carried me over to the bedroom. He laid me down and leaned over me.

"You are the most wonderful woman in the world, Marcia. You are the most wonderful woman in my life, Mrs. Tucker."

I thrilled to hear those words.

"Mrs. Tucker," I said. "I never believed I would ever have that name."

"You deserve it. You deserve everything I can give you."

"Take off your clothes, Mr. Tucker."

He moved back and slowly undressed. By the time he was naked, he had that wonderful erection back again.

"I love your penis," I said. "That's something I never thought I would say."

"I love what you do with it. I love your body. I love your breasts. I love your tummy. I love your vagina."

"Come here, you wonderful man."

He leaned over the bed and I reached out and took his penis in my hand. I rubbed it and felt all the familiar bumps and ridges. I looked at the tip and saw the juices of his love for me seeping out of the tiny hole.

"I want to do you with my mouth," I said. "Lay down."

"I get to go down on you, too."

"Can you get to me through all these clothes?"

"I can get to you through anything."

He lay down on his side, as did I and I took his penis into my mouth. He moved the layers of dress and petticoats and I felt his soft tongue touch my most sensitive parts. I nearly stopped licking him, it felt so wonderful. He worked so hard when he went down on me. He was obsessed with making me come when he did that. I kept moving my mouth up and down and licked along the entire length of his erection. He licked my clitoris and moved his finger up inside me. I wasn't going to last long. I could feel the culmination coming very soon.

I put my mouth over the end of his hard penis waiting for the wonderful finish of Ed's loving work. I could feel his tongue. I could feel his lips. I could feel his fingers working the juices around my vagina and labia. I could feel my excitement growing, and growing. Then, with that now familiar crash in my ears, I fell over the edge and came. My hips moved involuntarily. My legs closed around Ed's head, holding him to my hot crotch. I must have crushed his head between my thighs. My mouth rammed down around his erection, taking it all the way in, down my throat. I was out of control. I didn't even gag. I just swallowed his wonderful penis as far as I could. Then I felt his hips move and he came, pouring his wonderful fluid inside my throat. I sucked and sucked. Semen ran down my throat. Semen ran out of my mouth and down my chin. I loved it.

"I need you inside me," I was saying, breathlessly. I was desperate for his penis to enter me. I had to feet that hot hardness open me up and fill my insides. Slowly, Ed untangled himself from my skirts, petticoats, and legs. He turned me over carefully and began unbuttoning my dress.

"Please, Ed, come inside me."

I reached out to him and pulled him down to me. He resisted and I pulled harder, pulling his mouth down to mine, kissing him with all my passion.

"Let me undress you."

"Ed, I need you inside me."

"And I want to be inside you. Let me see you naked. I want to see your beautiful body beneath me when we make love."

I looked up at Ed. He was so handsome. His eyes showed nothing but love for me. His body was so perfect. His penis was already engorging, getting ready for the moment I could not wait for. I just lay there limply allowing him to lovingly undress me. He helped me out of the dress and then out of the petticoats. I was laying there in my garters, hose, and corset. He unlaced the corset and my breasts sprang free for the first time since early this morning. They ached for his hands and mouth. He slipped my shoes off then my garters and hose.

I was naked beneath my new husband. He looked at me lying there, so vulnerable, so desirable. My breasts were just for him. My vagina was just for him. My whole body, lying exposed under his gaze, just for him. He rubbed my belly with his hand. He licked my nipples. I shivered as I always shivered when he did that. He looked down at me lying underneath him. I looked back up at him and blew him a kiss. He leaned down and kissed me. Then, ever so slowly, he moved over me and in an instant his wonderful manhood slipped inside my womanhood. I was in love all over again.

He slid his penis in and out ever so slowly and lovingly. I moved my hips to match his movements. I could hear the sexy sound of our juices combining inside my vagina as he pulled nearly all the way out then slowly pushed all the way in. He covered my mouth with his. I wrapped my legs around his waist, holding myself to him, not letting him get away for even a second. I just wanted to have that man inside me forever. I just wanted to come together forever. I just wanted him to love me forever.

Afterword

I wrote The House on Sackett Street six years ago, not long after I married Ed. I was still very much a newly wed and very much into the amorous aspects of marriage, sex, and my new life. Things have matured and I now see things from a different perspective. Ed and I are still very much in love and we make just as passionate love as we did seven years ago when we met. I guess I just don't need to write about it as much.

As I write this, I am sitting in my new house, no longer on Sackett Street. I have a wonderful family. My husband, Ed, my daughter, Emily, a new baby son, and even a cat and a small dog keep me company and certainly keep me busy.

Ed still works downtown and I still write, publishing articles in various magazines every so often and even one short romance novel. It is still very hard to imagine all that I have gone through during these past years. My daughter is nearly seven, now, and doing quite well in school. My son, still an infant, still nursing, takes a lot of my time. Even so, I have been able to go back to school and take one or two courses to help me with my writing.

My new house is not far from Sackett Street, and not far from Debbie's home. Debbie lives by herself, now, the children having both moved away to college. I see her often, both at church and otherwise. We are very close, although not as close as I wrote in this story. We see each other as sisters, now, although, I must admit, that we have sampled each other's wares on occasion, just for memory's sake.

So, has it all been worth it? Has the loss of one life and the changes wrought upon other lives been worth the pain of the change? Perhaps. I am happy, although there are times when I wonder what would have happened to my service career had I been able to keep going. I wonder how my life as a father and husband would have been. I wonder how my relationship with my son and daughter would have been.

While Ed, Debbie, and my children are fully aware of all that has occurred, things can never be completely normal. As it is now, I am a relatively unknown author, writing short stories and trying to break into the romance novel market. It's hard, but it has been rewarding. I have been able to raise a beautiful daughter who would have been abused or otherwise have had a bad life. I have been able to live with a wonderful partner who has taken care of me and who loves me dearly. Would I do it all over again? Probably not, but given the circumstances that led me to the decision, I have no regrets. I am fifty years old, now. I am a respected woman in the life of our church. I am the respected mother of Emily and recognized as an authority on some issues at the local parent teacher organization. I have done well, and, God willing will continue so to do. I offer my best wishes to those who have great expectations, as well as to those who have great expectations thrust upon them.

Printed in Great Britain
by Amazon.co.uk, Ltd.,
Marston Gate.